CHARLESTON'S
NAVY YARD

Coker Craft Press, Inc.
P. O. Box 176
Charleston, S. C. 29402

© 1985 by Jim McNeil. All rights reserved.

Printed in the United States of America

    by The R. L. Bryan Co., Columbia, S. C.

Library of Congress Cataloging-in-Publication Data

McNeil, Jim, 1942-
    Charleston's navy yard.

    Includes index.
    1. Charleston Naval Shipyard — History.
    2. Charleston (S. C.) — History, Naval.
    I. Title. VA70.C4M38 1985   359.7′5′09757915   85-29030

ISBN 0-914432-02-8

CHARLESTON'S NAVY YARD

a picture history

BY JIM McNEIL

Published by
CokerCraft Press
Charleston, S. C.

To Sylvia, Sean, Wendy,
Tracy, and Chris

State of South Carolina

Office of the Governor

RICHARD W. RILEY
GOVERNOR

POST OFFICE BOX 11450
COLUMBIA 29211

The development of the Charleston Navy Yard is a period of South Carolina history in which all South Carolinians should take pride. From the earliest Colonial times through the nuclear age, Charleston has served as a focal point for building and maintaining a strong merchant and military fleet. Throughout this nation's history, there have been times when sacrifices and contributions had to be made. This is the theme of <u>Charleston's Navy Yard: A Picture History</u>. Using concrete facts complemented by rich pictures, Jim McNeil has thoughtfully examined the impact of Charleston's shipbuilding efforts on this State and nation.

I have often said that the people of South Carolina were patriotic, industrious, and far sighted. From the gift of the Chicora Park site to the thriving partnership between the City of Charleston and the Navy Yard today, these traits are self-evident.

I would finally like to add my congratulations to the fine author and publisher of this work. It is a fine addition to the historical research on this state which adds so much to our life in South Carolina.

Richard W. Riley

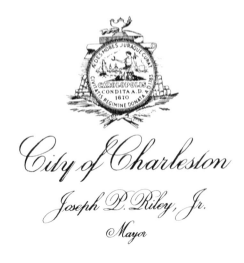

City of Charleston

Joseph P. Riley, Jr.
Mayor

My congratulations are extended to Jim McNeil and others responsible for publishing Charleston's Navy Yard: A Picture History. This book develops in a most interesting way a fascinating chapter of Charleston's rich history. The first settling of the property, the development of Chicora Park, the conceptualization and creation of the Charleston Navy Yard and its extraordinary development in modern times makes for interesting reading. Certainly the Charleston Naval Shipyard has exceeded the fondest hopes and dreams of those responsible for its creation. We are proud of the role that is played in the defense of our nation, the sophisticated technological advancements that are represented there and, of course, the thousands of people who have worked and are working in the Navy Yard.

I have often been interested in its history and have admired the many beautifully designed industrial buildings that still stand. This book also points out an all-but-forgotten fact of the City of Charleston's role in the development of the Naval Shipyard.

Charleston's Navy Yard, I am confident, will be an important research tool for historians and will be interesting reading for Charlestonians and those interested in this city's history.

Joseph P. Riley, Jr., Mayor
City of Charleston

P.O. Box 652, Charleston, South Carolina 29402 803-577-6970

JOHN E. BOURNE, JR.
Mayor

CITY COUNCIL
Pete B. Adams
James V. Edwards
Richard Ganaway
Don John Hays
Patsy W. Hughes
R. E. Zipperer

City of
North Charleston

SOUTH CAROLINA

Box 10100
North Charleston, S.C. 29411
Telephone 554-5700

I am pleased to have had an opportunity to review the history of the Charleston Naval Base and related facilities. While the Naval Shipyard precedes the City by many years, I think it is an obvious fact that without the facility being located in our community many of the things we presently enjoy would not have occurred. The Shipyard has rich heritage and enjoys an outstanding reputation among Federal Shipyards, and we are pleased that the facility, one of the major Federal Shipyards in the nation, is located within the corporate limits of our City.

Within days of the incorporation of the City of North Charleston, I met with Admiral Herman Kossler, Commandant of the 6th Naval District, to discuss with him the possibility of annexing the Naval Shipyard into the City of North Charleston. Eventually this did take place and represented one of our first major annexations; therefore, the Shipyard has been a part of our City almost from its inception. We have enjoyed a good relationship with both the civilian and military leadership at the Yard, and this relationship, I believe, has been beneficial to both sides. We will look forward to this continued good relationship as both the City and the Yard prosper.

I would like to especially commend those who had a part in putting together this very comprehensive document which outlines in great detail the activities and accomplishments of the Naval Shipyard.

Sincerely,

John E. Bourne, Jr.
Mayor

Contents

President Theodore Roosevelt gestures to Charleston Major J. Adger Smyth on board the revenue cutter Algonquin on a windy April day in 1902. Following his tour of the site of the new Navy Yard, the President visited Fort Sumter.

Prologue

It was a blustery April day in 1902. Charleston Mayor J. Adger Smyth was standing on the deck of the revenue cutter *Algonquin* in the Cooper River. At his side was the President of the United States who had just arrived in Charleston on his private train.

A few minutes before, Mayor Smyth had shown the President the site of the new Navy Yard on the west bank of the river a few miles above the city. To the north was Chicora Park, a favorite recreational spot where the mayor's own daughter had danced in the pavilion on warm summer evenings. To the south they could see an old plantation house standing among a clump of live oaks on the shore. The plantation had been called Marshlands, a name obviously still fitting for the area.

President Theodore Roosevelt, a student of history, could readily have visualized what it had been like a half-century before, with great rice fields like those of other plantations which once lined the river banks. But even a visionary such as Roosevelt could scarcely have imagined the Navy Yard four short decades later, when 25,000 workers would be turning out a new vessel every week and repairing ships fighting in a global war. Nor could he have foreseen a time when missile-firing submarines, as big as the cruisers of his day and powered by splitting atoms, would ply the tranquil waters of the Cooper River as plantation boats rowed by chanting slaves once did.

It was a fitting place for the nation's new Navy Yard, for Charleston had always been wedded to the sea. This relationship began with arrival of the first colonists in 1670 after a long and perilous ocean voyage. The settlers found a magnificent, easily-defended harbor formed by the Ashley and Cooper rivers. Here they built a great seaport which they found ample opportunity to defend; against French and Spanish invaders, against pirates, and finally against the Federal Navy during the Civil War.

From early in the eighteenth century Charleston was a busy port. Many of her ships were Charleston-built, carrying rice and furs and other goods to distant ports. Some were warships, such as the frigate *John Adams*, built in 1799 by the people of Charleston as a patriotic gift to the infant American Navy.

The Federal Navy tried to choke the life from Charleston during the Civil War with a tight blockade. Then early in the twentieth century the United States Navy provided the city's economic salvation with the great shipyard on the Cooper River.

Today, Charleston, North Charleston and the surrounding communities are the home of one of the world's great naval complexes and one of the finest shipyards in America, continuing the splendid naval tradition that began nearly three centuries ago in the days of William Rhett.

1

The Early Naval Tradition

From its very beginning, Charleston has been inexorably linked with the sea.

The town was founded because of the splendid harbor where the Ashley and Cooper rivers meet. In the eighteenth century it became one of the great American seaports — sending rice, indigo, animal skins and other products of the rich land of Carolina to England, the islands to the south, and the other American colonies.

It was the mother settlement of the colony; a city-state of wealthy planters from surrounding plantations, of great merchants such as Henry Laurens who traded in the staples of Carolina, of well-to-do tradesmen such as shipbuilder John Rose. It developed an elegant, cosmopolitan society much like that of London in the time of Charles II, the monarch for whom the town was named.

Despite the elegance of its society, the town was tough. It quickly learned not to rely on far-away England for its protection. His Majesty's men-of-war assigned to the Carolina station were few and far between.

The necessity for self-reliance fostered an independent spirit. Because of Charleston's close association with the sea, this independence led to a remarkable naval tradition — a tradition not of one navy, but of four.

The first was a provincial navy of colonial times, raised by the governor when the town was in peril. Next came the South Carolina Navy of the Revolution. A generation later, at the end of the eighteenth century, Charleston[1] was building ships for the new American Navy and manning them with "brave tars."

But the patriotic pride in the new republic gradually died in Charleston, mainly over the issue of slavery on which the city and state so much depended. It was replaced by an isolationist spirit and a

---

[1] The city was originally named Charles Towne, then later Charlestowne, often spelled without the final e. In 1783, the name was officially changed to Charleston. For the sake of simplicity, the name *Charleston* is used throughout this book regardless of the time period.

In 1695 when this fine map was drawn, Charleston was already twenty-five years old. On the east bank of the Wando River can be seen the residence of George Dearsley, one of Charleston's early shipbuilders. For more than two centuries, the great sand bar at the mouth of the harbor was as important to the defense of the city as her forts. Crossing Charleston bar in a large vessel was a slow process, requiring careful soundings and best done with the aid of a local pilot. Courtesy the Charleston Museum

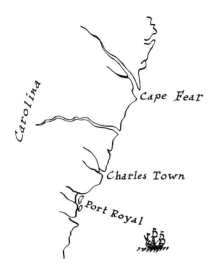

The original colonists planned to settle at Port Royal, some fifty miles to the south of Charleston. After landing there they were persuaded to move north to the site on the Ashley River by an Indian known as the Cassique of the Kiawah.

growing independence that finally led to civil war. Thus, the fourth navy of early Charleston became the Confederate Navy. And Charleston Harbor became the scene of battles between Confederate vessels and Federal warships that live in naval history.

Charleston first raised a navy in 1706. It was during the time of Queen Anne's War when England was at war with France and Spain. As the southernmost English stronghold on the Atlantic seaboard, the town had been expecting an attack from the enemies of the mother country. On Saturday, 24 August 1706, the invaders came.

Off the bar appeared five French vessels, a frigate and four sloops from Havana that had picked up a force of Spanish soldiers at St. Augustine. The town was alerted when a lookout on Sullivan's Island spotted the enemy and lit "five smokes," the prearranged signal indicating the number of vessels off the coast. Governor Nathaniel Johnson, who was at his plantation Silk Hope on the Cooper River, was sent for. Colonel William Rhett rallied the militia. The French Fleet, in the meantime, spent the next day sounding the bar looking for a safe passage.

When the French finally entered the harbor, the fortifications of the town appeared too menacing for direct attack. The fleet instead anchored off Sullivan's Island. On Wednesday, the 28th, an ultimatum to surrender was sent to the governor which was steadfastly refused. The next day, the French commander dispatched raiding parties to James Island and the area north of Sullivan's Island.

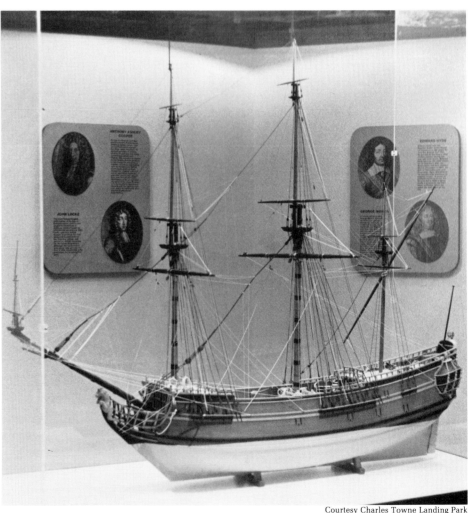

In 1669, the colonists left England for Carolina in three ships; only the Carolina, at about 100-tons burden the largest of the vessels, finally made it. This model of her can be seen at Charles Towne Landing Park, located at the site of the original settlement on the Ashley River.

Courtesy Charles Towne Landing Park

Meanwhile, Governor Johnson had commissioned Rhett as vice admiral of the colony and Rhett had assembled the vessels in the harbor and had them armed and made ready for sea. These vessels, the first Charleston navy, consisted of three ships, a brigantine, two sloops, and a craft loaded with combustibles which served as a fireship.

On Saturday morning, 31 August, the little fleet sailed out into the harbor to meet the enemy. However, to the surprise of the colonists, not a shot was exchanged. Instead, the French vessels weighed anchor, crossed the bar and headed for sea. One of the French vessels was later captured by Rhett a few miles north of Charleston at Sewee Bay.

Twelve years later, the town again assembled small fleets of armed vessels, this time to deal with pirates who were plundering shipping off the coast. The first, once more commanded by Colonel Rhett, captured the infamous Stede Bonnet at Cape Fear. The second, led by the governor himself, engaged the pirate vessel of the notorious Richard Worley. Worley and a number of his men were killed and the rest of his crew taken back to the town to hang.

The second Charleston navy was assembled not to deal with pirates or the enemies of the mother country, but with England herself. As did ten of the other colonies, South Carolina raised her own navy during the early years of the American Revolution.

During the American Revolution, South Carolina had her own navy as did many of the other states. This painting by William Nowland Van Powell shows the ship Prosper, the brig Comet and the schooner Defense at Rebellion Road in Charleston Harbor in 1775. These vessels were among the earliest taken into the State Navy.

Courtesy Robert Sanderson, Williamsburg, Va.

The South Carolina Navy, with Charleston as its base of operations, was assembled and managed by a board of commissioners consisting of eight local citizens. Alexander Gillion, a leading merchant of the town, was appointed commodore. Vessels belonging to local shipowners, such as the 20-gun ship *Prosper*, were taken into service. Some, such as the 14-gun brig *Hornet*, were built in Charleston at the direction of the Navy Board. The State Navy had some of the finest vessels in American service during the Revolution, including the big Dutch-built frigate *South Carolina* and the 44-gun ship *Bricole*. In all, more than thirty vessels saw service in the State Navy. Privateers were also commissioned by the state to raid British shipping. The best known of these was the 14-gun snow *Fair American* whose beautiful model, made by the British not long after the Revolution, can be seen today at the museum of the U. S. Naval Academy.

The South Carolina Navy was deployed mainly against British shipping, off the Carolina and Florida coasts and in the West Indies, and in the defense of Charleston. Most of the vessels were commanded by local sea captains, such as Robert Cochran of the brig *Notre Dame*. Able seamen were in short supply in the local area and in 1776 Cochran journeyed to Massachusetts to recruit 300 men for the State Navy. Four years later, on 12 May 1780, the South Carolina Navy was no more, the vessels sunk or captured as Charleston fell into British hands.

Shown here in Marseille Harbor, the 44-gun Bricole *and the 28-gun* Truitt *were obtained from France for service in the South Carolina Navy.*

William Nowland Van Powell painting courtesy Robert Sanderson, Williamsburg, Va.

Courtesy Naval Academy Museum.

This beautiful model of the 16-gun snow Fair American was made by the British some years after the Revolution. Fair American served as a privateer in the South Carolina Navy, one of a number given letters of marque by the state to sail against British shipping. A snow like her differed from a brig by having a third mast, just behind the main mast, which carried the aft sail or "driver".

The fine craftsmanship of the Naval Academy model is evident in this view. A ship named Fair American had been built in Carolina in 1761, of "oak from Coffin Island", the Folly Island of today. There is no evidence, however, that these two were the same vessel.

Photograph and model from the collection of the United States Naval Academy Museum.

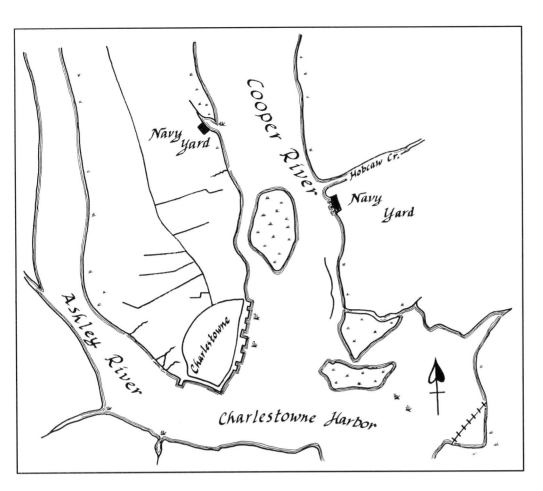

To maintain the vessels of the State Navy, the Navy Commissioners of South Carolina set up two navy yards. The first was the shipyard on Charleston Neck, leased from Robert Cochran in 1777. The following year, a major portion of Paul Pritchard's big shipyard at Hobcaw was purchased by the commissioners and Pritchard hired to manage the operation.

The Continental frigate Randolph was a frequent visitor to Charleston Harbor in 1777 and 1778. This painting by William Nowland Van Powell shows her in September of 1777 in the Cooper River, just south of the Exchange. The occasion was a reception for a Charlestowne girl betrothed to her captain, Nicholas Biddle. On 7 March 1778, Randolph, accompanied by Notredame, Fair American, General Moultrie and Polly of the South Carolina Navy, encountered the British 64-gun ship Yarmouth. In the ensuing battle, Randolph's magazine exploded, completely destroying the ship. Only four of the 215-man crew survived.

The second most powerful warship in the South Carolina Navy, and perhaps the finest vessel in American service during the Revolution, was the big 40-gun frigate South Carolina. She was built in Amsterdam in 1777 to a French design as L'Indien. One authority says that Joshua Humphreys, who had a plan of the ship in his personal notebook, may have used her as inspiration in design of the Constitution class of frigates.

The brig Notre Dame of the South Carolina Navy was first commanded by Robert Cochran. Cochran was the leading sea captain in Charleston for many years after the Revolution.

Peabody Museum of Salem.

William Nowland Van Powell painting courtesy of Robert Sanderson.

Following the Revolution, what was left of the Continental Navy and those of the states were disbanded and the ships sold or broken up. The United States had no navy until the fall of 1797 when the *United States*, the *Constellation* and the *Constitution*, the first of the six frigates authorized by the Congress in 1794, were launched. In 1798 and 1799, the *Constitution* and the *Constellation* frequently passed off Charleston bar as they escorted convoys of merchantmen from New England to the West Indies and back.

Actually, Charlestonians had plans to build a naval vessel well before this. In January of 1794, efforts were made to raise money to build a frigate for naval service. Five years later, the 28-gun frigate *John Adams*, built and paid for by the people of Charleston, was turned over to the new American Navy as the sixth most powerful vessel in the fleet.

In the last years of the eighteenth century, during the undeclared naval war with France, there was a flurry of naval shipbuilding in the United States. Charleston did her share with vessels like the 187-ton topsail schooner *South Carolina*, the brig *General Pinckney* and several armed galleys for coastal defense, as well as the splendid frigate *John Adams*.

In the early years of the nineteenth century, gunboats and other naval vessels were built at Charleston. However, after the War of 1812 none were built for more than a century, until the Charleston Navy Yard was established. None, that is, except for warships of the Confederate Navy.

Numerous ocean-going vessels were built in Charleston in the early years and many were named South Carolina, *including this sperm whaling ship completed in 1815.*

The Peabody Museum of Salem.

In April of 1861, the Civil War began in Charleston Harbor. It began with the Confederacy ill-prepared to fight a naval war, in fact with no navy at all.

Taking advantage of the situation, President Lincoln declared a naval blockade of Southern ports. A massive blockading fleet was assembled. At Charleston, Union efforts included an attempt to block passage into the harbor by sinking old whaling ships — the "Stone Fleet" — in the main shipping channel.

Early in the war the Federal blockade was ineffective. Daring blockade runners left Charleston loaded with cotton and returned with war materials and supplies obtained from Bermuda and Nassau. Later the blockade tightened, causing severe shortages in Charleston of nearly everything.

Charlestonians responded with typical resourcefulness and ingenuity to build warships to combat the Federal fleet. As many as a score of Confederate naval vessels were constructed at Charleston during the years of the war. These included big ironclad rams such as the *Chicora*, the *Palmetto State* and the *Charleston*. The spar torpedo boat *Little David* and many others like her were built, as well as the great ironclad *Columbia*. During this period, any suitable vessel was pressed into service for the Confederacy, ships such as the steamer *Marion* built in Charleston in 1850 and the *Planter*, a 313-ton steamer built the year before the war — the vessel turned over to the Union Navy by her Negro pilot in 1862.

The engagements between Confederate vessels and Union warships in Charleston Harbor opened a new era in naval warfare.

A well-known Charleston architect invented the spar torpedo, an explosive charge carried on a long pole attached to the bow of an attacking vessel. In 1863, this device was used by the *Little David*, a strange vessel shaped "like a long Segar," to damage the huge Federal ironclad warship *New Ironsides* in the world's first successful torpedo attack. The next year the Confederate submarine *H. L. Hunley* used the same device to sink the *Housatonic*, a big Union steam-powered sloop-of-war. *H. L. Hunley*'s exploit was the first time a submarine had ever sunk a warship in combat.

Despite the innovative vessels and the efforts of their brave crews, Charleston fell in February of 1865 as the Confederate forces evacuated the city before the advance of Sherman's armies. The war left destruction and poverty in its wake, and a harbor filled with shipwrecks.

John Smith painting courtesy of the Citadel Museum.

In the last years of the eighteenth century, the new American frigate Constitution frequently passed off Charleston bar while escorting convoys of merchant ships from New England to the West Indies and on their return voyage.

The Year of The Pirates

Pirates began to visit Charleston in the early years of the colony. Their gold and silver, freely spent in the town, made them welcome for many years.

More than a century later, Edmund Genét, the French minister, was in the city recruiting privateersmen to sail against the enemies of the French Republic. In the early 1790s, the French raiders made Charleston their main operating base in America. Privateersmen parading through the streets with long sabres at their sides were a common sight. But in more than a century of pirate activity, nothing matched the year 1718 — the year of the pirates.

It started with Edward Teach, the notorious Blackbeard. In May of 1718, commanding a fleet of four armed vessels, he blockaded Charleston Harbor — taking every ship that dared venture past the bar. His crew needed medicines which he demanded from Governor Johnson, threatening to send the heads of hostages he had taken if his demands were not met. Governor Robert Johnson, whose father had rallied the town against the French and Spanish fleet in 1706, had little choice but to give in. After receiving the medical supplies, Blackbeard released the hostages, stripped of their possessions, and moved on to North Carolina.

On board Blackbeard's *Queen Anne's Revenge* at the time was another notorious pirate, Stede Bonnet. Known as the Gentleman Pirate, Bonnet had started piracy in a unique fashion. Supposedly driven by a nagging wife, the well-educated, former British Army officer had bought a sloop, armed her and hired a crew. He named the vessel *Revenge* and sailed north from Barbados in early 1717 in search of ships to plunder. After considerable success at his new profession, he joined with Blackbeard for a time — an association he quickly regretted as the stronger Teach took over his vessel. They later parted company after both received the King's pardon from Governor Eden of North Carolina.

Bonnet's resolve to quit pirating weakened rapidly. He changed the name of his sloop to *Royal James*, started calling himself Captain Thomas, and returned to his former ways. However, in August of 1718 the *Royal James* was beginning to leak and badly needed careening to remove sea growth from the bottom of her hull. He put in at the mouth of the Cape Fear River, at the site of present day Southport, to make repairs.

Shortly afterwards, word reached Charleston that a pirate ship was laid up at Cape Fear. By this time, Governor Johnson was fed up with pirates harassing Charleston shipping. Colonel William Rhett volunteered to pursue the pirates and was put in charge of two armed sloops, the *Sea Nymph* and the *Henry*.

As they were being readied for sea, it was reported that the pirate Charles Vane was outside the bar. Rhett's vessels first searched for Vane unsuccessfully and then turned northward for Cape Fear. On 28 September 1718, they arrived and promptly ran aground within sight of the *Royal James*. At dawn the next morning, a bloody battle began that ended in the capture of Bonnet and his men. Rhett brought them back to Charleston where they were imprisoned awaiting trial. Bonnet escaped — in woman's clothing it was said — but was soon recaptured by Colonel

Carolina Art Association, Gibbes Art Gallery, Charleston, S. C.

Colonel William Rhett was the military strongman of the early colony. In 1706, commissioned by the governor as vice admiral of the province, he raised a fleet of seven vessels and chased the invading French Fleet from the harbor. Twelve years later, he captured the pirate Stede Bonnet at Cape Fear.

Rhett on Sullivan's Island. Bonnet and most of his crew were hanged at White Point and their bodies buried below the highwater mark.

Even as Bonnet was in prison awaiting trial, another pirate, Richard Worley, began plundering shipping off Charleston bar. This time Governor Johnson took matters in his own hands. He assembled a fleet of four ships including the *Royal James* and engaged Worley's vessel. In the ensuing battle, Worley was killed and all his crewmen killed or captured.

While pirates sailed the southern waters for many years afterwards, most stayed well away from Charleston.

Today, there are still reminders in Charleston of the year of the pirates. Walk down Hasell Street and you can see Colonel Rhett's old plantation house. Several blocks south in the cemetery of St. Philip's lies his grave. Go just around the corner and you'll see the house of Chief Justice Nicholas Trott who sentenced Bonnet to hang. And on the Battery at White Point, you can see a marker where Bonnet and his men swung from the gallows — some were left there for days to remind would-be pirates of Charleston justice.

From *A General History of the Pirates* by Capt. Charles Johnson, the Cayne Press, 1925. The Mariner's Museum, Newport News, Va.

In June of 1718, Edward Teach, the fearsome Blackbeard, blockaded Charleston Harbor, taking every ship that dared venture across the bar. Also aboard his flagship, the Queen Anne's Revenge, was Stede Bonnet, the gentleman pirate. Blackbeard was killed later that year by an expedition sent out by Governor Spotwood of Virginia.

From *A General History of the Pirates* by Capt. Charles Johnson. The Mariner's Museum.

This illustration, first published in 1724, shows a merchant ship under attack by the vessel of Charles Vane. Vane was one of the pirates who plagued Charleston waters in the early years of the eighteenth century.

From *A General History of the Pirates* by Capt. Charles Johnson, the Cayne Press, 1925. The Mariner's Museum, Newport News, Va.

Bonnet's vessel, the Royal James, put in at Cape Fear in August of 1718 for repairs. Word reached Charleston shortly afterwards that a pirate ship was laid up on the river there. Colonel William Rhett volunteered to pursue the pirates and was put in charge of two armed sloops, the Sea Nymph and the Henry. On 29 September 1718, the bloody battle took place that resulted in the capture of Bonnet and his surviving men.

River of Plantations

In 1685, a brigantine sailing from Madagascar put into Charleston for repairs. Aboard the vessel was a small quantity of rice which the captain gave to Dr. Henry Woodward, the first English settler of the colony. Dr. Woodward and others planted the rice which in later years became known as Carolina Gold, the finest rice in all the world.

The land for planting was cheap, a mere penny an acre, and the Lords Proprietors of the colony provided titles of nobility to large land-owners. Before long, great rice plantations lined the banks of the rivers of the Carolina Lowcountry. Rice and, for a time, indigo were grown in enormous quantities and loaded at Charleston on ships bound for England, the West Indies and the other American colonies.

Carolina Gold was grown by people the planters called their "black gold" — slaves brought by the hundreds from Africa and the West Indies. Besides being good workers, the Negroes were immune to malaria, which afflicted the white settlers. During the summer months, the plantation owners and their families lived in their Charleston townhouses to escape the dreaded fever.

From the time of the early settlement, a path used by Indians and traders led west from Charleston all the way to the Mississippi. But the rivers were the highways of those times. Plantation owners came to Charleston in long boats made of cypress logs and rowed by chanting slaves. Later, the coming of the steamboat made river travel faster and more convenient, making it possible to travel from Charleston to the upper reaches of the Cooper River and return in a single day.

One frequent traveler of the river in ante-bellum years was Dr. John B. Irving. Dr. Irving was a Charleston physician and owner of a rice plantation on the Cooper. He loved the river and left a vivid description of what it was like in 1842.

Try to imagine how it was then, riding the steamboat with Dr. Irving as it chugged up the river through the early morning mists. Hooves clattering on cobblestones as you drive to the wharf through the dark streets. The boatman taking your dollar as you step on board. The barnyard smells and sounds of livestock already on the steamer.

As the boat pulls away from the wharf, you have a splendid view of the city. The rising sun painting with gold the steeples of St. Michael's and the Circular Church. Smoke drifting from a score of chimneys. The lofty masts of vessels in the Cooper shining in the sunlight. The harbor coming alive with small boats moving about among the bigger vessels like lazy birds.

Stand on the port side and look toward the shore. Passing the Charleston Neck you can see the white brick buildings of the state arsenal, designed by Robert Mills, a Charleston son then the federal architect in Washington. Next comes Magnolia Umbra, the plantation where Magnolia

Just to the south of the old shipyard on Charleston Neck was Belvidere Plantation. This house was built there around 1800. It served as the club house for the Charleston Country Club early in this century.

Carolina Art Association, Gibbes Art Gallery

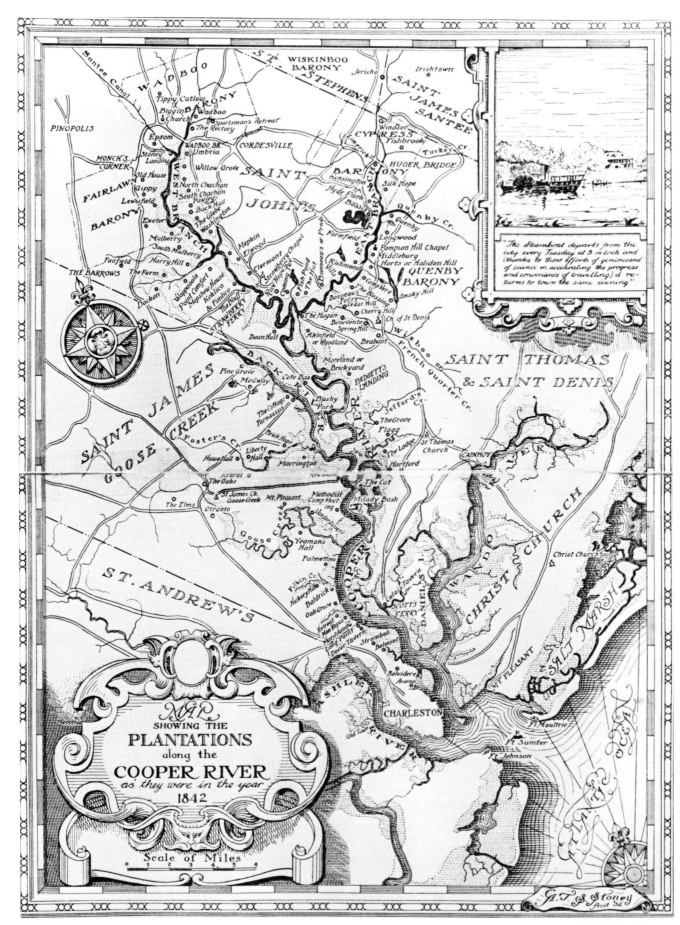

MAP
SHOWING THE
PLANTATIONS
along the
COOPER RIVER
as they were in the year
1842

Scale of Miles

"The Steamboat departs from the city every Tuesday at 5 o'clock and (thanks to those efforts of genius and of science in accelerating the progress and convenience of travelling) it returns to town the same evening"

16

Cemetery, Charleston's huge Victorian graveyard, would be started in a few years. You and Dr. Irving would then see the Belvidere Rice Mill and the big plantation house "lying amid green fields and meadows." Ask Dr. Irving who lived there and he would tell you it was once the home of Governor Robert Johnson and later of Colonel Tom Shubrick. Dr. Irving was a fine storyteller and he could tell you that here Colonel Shubrick's wife had strange dreams of her husband being lost at sea — dreams so vivid that she sent a search party to look for him. He was found, amazingly enough, in Bulls Bay, clinging to a chicken coop washed from the deck of his perished vessel.

After you pass the fields of Belvidere, you see the mouth of the big creek. It had been known by many names — such as Long Point Creek for the old plantation to the north and Cochran's Creek for the sea captain who had a shipyard there. Here Paul Pritchard, Jr. built the frigate *John Adams* in 1799. The creek would be called Shipyard Creek in memory of the early shipbuilding on its banks.

The paddle wheels beat through the still water as the river bends to the left. You can see the ruins of Dover Tavern and its dilapidated landing surrounded by the marsh. Crossing off the bow of your steamer is a strange-looking contraption, a little mule-powered ferryboat which has just left the Charleston side of the river.

In the distance, you see black men and women working in the rice fields. Then you see an immense white plantation house. This is Marshlands and belongs to Nathaniel Heyward, the wealthiest rice planter in the Carolinas. According to Dr. Irving, "It contains a large quantity of very valuable rice land, and annually sends good crops to market." One hundred and twenty years later the plantation house would be moved so a huge dry dock could be built to overhaul submarines that could send rockets across the sea.

Continuing up the river, you pass two more plantations. The first is called the Retreat — in a few years, Andrew Turnbull would buy the property and build a fine plantation house. A half-century later, the city of Charleston would build a beautiful recreation park here. The next plantation is Oak Grove. The creek that forms the southern boundary of the property would be called Noisette Creek for Paul Noisette who bought the plantation in 1865.

And so it was in 1842, as the steamboat journeyed up the Cooper River. Two short decades later, Charleston Harbor would be blockaded by the Union fleet and the city under siege. With the war would die the old plantation way of life.

For sixty years until it was moved to Fort Johnson to make room for Dry Dock 5, the historic Marshlands Plantation house was a unique feature of the yard. The house was built in 1810 or shortly thereafter by the rice planter John Ball. It is notable for lovely woodwork, particularly over the interior doors. In 1925, photographs of the interior were made to use in remodeling the White House. In the early years of the Navy Yard, the house was used for administrative offices and those of draftsmen and the civil engineer.

In 1842, the Cooper was truly a river of plantations. The site where the Navy Yard would be built was then occupied by the plantations of Marshlands, Mon Repos, and the Retreat. Long Point, to the south, was an older plantation. Belvidere, south of Shipyard Creek, was once the plantation of Governor Robert Johnson who helped rid Charleston of pirates in 1718.

Hearts of Oak

Ships were built at Charleston in the early years of the colony more than three centuries ago. By the time of the American Revolution, a sizeable shipbuilding industry had developed, centered at Hobcaw on the Wando River.

During the eighteenth century, most of the vessels built were schooners, generally small, two-masted craft of less than fifty tons. Also built were larger square-rigged vessels: brigs, carrying square sails on two masts; snows, a variation of the brig; and three-masted square-rigged vessels known as ships.

In 1753, a great shipyard was established at Hobcaw by two Scotsmen, James Stewart and John Rose, who became the leading shipbuilders of Charleston.

Stewart arrived in the city in 1749 from the Woolwich Naval Yard near London, where he had served as an apprentice to his uncle Mungo Murray, a leading English shipwright. His partner, John Rose, an "Honest, Sensible man" according to Charleston merchant Henry Laurens, was the son of a Scotsman known as Hugh Rose of Clava. John Rose also became a wealthy and respected member of Charleston society.

The yard of Stewart and Rose became the biggest in the colony. It was located on the Wando River, between Hobcaw Creek and Molasses Creek. Spread out over more than a hundred acres, it was a large shipyard for the period, with "very Substantial good Wharves and Other Conveniences Sufficient to Heave down Three Vessels at the same time." Typical of the larger vessels constructed there was the *Heart of Oak*, a ship of 180 tons launched in 1763. Rose owned her himself. Her first voyage was to London, carrying 1,000 barrels of Carolina rice. Rose went as a passenger to recruit British shipwrights for his yard — for qualified ship carpenters were often in short supply in South Carolina.

There were other yards at Hobcaw as well. In 1769, the local newspaper reported "a fine new ship, for the London trade, was launched at Captain Lempriere's at Hobcaw . . . and is expected to be as compleat a Vessel as has been built in this Province; She is called *Betsy and Elfy.*" Clement Lempriere's shipyard was at Lempriere's Point, next to the yard of Stewart and Rose on the Wando.

Charleston vessels were built of the finest woods. Carolina live oak, used for frames and other structural members, was hard and tough and, when properly cured, exceptionally durable — qualities soon recognized by British builders. In 1771, the Carolina-built *Fair American* was lengthened in the graving dock of an English yard. She was a ten-year-old ship that had seen hard service hauling rice to Liverpool. Roger Fisher, the shipwright in charge of the work, was so impressed with the live oak of which her frame was made that he wrote a letter to the Admiralty, praising it as stronger and better than British oak. The timbers in *Fair American* had come from "Coffin Island, at the entrance of Charles Town bar," the Folly Island of today.

Another wood used extensively by Charleston shipbuilders was yellow pine. The tall, straight, long-leaf pine trees in the Lowcountry made fine masts and spars. Pine was also used for the planking, or strakes as they are called, of the hull and for decks and bulkheads within the ship.

Charleston vessels were also known for being well-built. Then, as now, however, the cost of construction and the ability to finish a vessel on time were important to both the customer and the builder's reputation. Take the case of the *Dependence*, a small, finely-crafted schooner-rigged pilot boat built in Charleston for the governor of East Florida in 1765.

Henry Laurens had her built to the governor's specifications at the yard of Charles Minors. The eminent Charleston merchant, who did much to promote shipbuilding in South Carolina, found acting as the governor's agent to be a painful ordeal. The vessel cost more than planned and was completed late. In a letter explaining this situation to the governor, the frustrated Laurens referred to the builder as "that almost insensible crabbed Creature." Minors and his shipwrights, Laurens called "a pack of damned Pick Pockets." Laurens also allowed that he had ordered "one of the Fellows to a place reputed to be hotter than Savannah." He did begrudgingly admit to the governor that the vessel was "clever, well put together, &ca." in the tradition of Charleston shipbuilders.

In 1769, the Hobcaw shipyard of Stewart and Rose was sold to William Begbie and Daniel Manson. Begbie and Manson continued operation of the yard until a short time prior to the start of the American Revolution when the yard was purchased by Paul Pritchard.

Pritchard had arrived in Charleston from Northern Ireland in 1766. For a quarter century he was one of the leading shipbuilders of the city. He built vessels at his yard at Hobcaw and also at the shipyard on Charleston Neck, which he leased from Robert Cochran.

A few years prior to the Revolution, the shipyard on Charleston Neck was established by Cochran on property inherited by his wife, Mary Elliott. The shipyard was located on the south side of Shipyard Creek, just to the north of Belvidere Plantation. Cochran was one of Charleston's best-known sea captains and was active in establishing the South Carolina Navy.

In 1777, the Commissioners of the State Navy leased Cochran's yard to maintain and repair the vessels of their fleet. This arrangement proved unsatisfactory, however. For one thing, the yard was small; there was little space for storage and the wharf could handle only one vessel at a time. For another, it was too close to Charleston and its attractions. Just a good walk or a short coach ride away, the taverns of the town proved too great a temptation. The Navy Commissioners quickly found that "people belonging to the Yard, as well as the Sailors belonging to the vessels do Frequently come to Town, get Drunk and quit the Service. . . ."

Faced with these difficulties, the commissioners decided to move the yard to Hobcaw. In October of 1778, they bought eighty-five acres of Paul Pritchard's yard, about three-fourths of his property, and hired the renowned shipbuilder to manage the operation. They were impressed with Pritchard's qualifications, recognizing him as "a Man of Property, an Experienced Ship Wright" who "understands the management of Negroes." The latter quality was considered particularly important because slaves did much of the work on Charleston-built vessels of that period, and many were skilled shipwrights. The South Carolina Navy Yard remained at Hobcaw until May of 1780 when Charleston fell into British hands.

When Paul Pritchard died in 1791, his business passed to his son, Paul Pritchard, Jr., who continued the family tradition. In the last years of the eighteenth century, Paul Pritchard, Jr. built several vessels at the shipyard on Charleston Neck. These included the 187-ton revenue schooner *South Carolina*, launched in November of 1798, and the 28-gun frigate *John Adams*, Charleston's gift to the infant American navy, which went to sea a year later.

Shipbuilding was often a family business in Charleston. "Hobcaw Bill" Pritchard, the elder Paul's brother, was also a shipwright. Paul Pritchard III carried on the family business, and constructed an ill-fated steamer that exploded in Charleston Harbor in 1826.

Another Charleston shipbuilding family was that of James Marsh. Young Marsh was the foreman of Pritchard's yard when the *John Adams* was built in 1798 and 1799. Marsh had just moved to town from Perth Amboy, New Jersey and this was his first job in Charleston.

Marsh later established his own shipyard on Concord Street where the *General Pinckney* had been built, just north of where the United States Customs House now stands. He eventually jointly owned the business with his son, James Marsh, Jr. In the middle of the nineteenth century, they built and operated a floating dry dock here, the first in Charleston. The dry dock was moored at the foot of Hayne Street.

James Marsh, at his death in 1852, owned five houses on East Bay Street near the shipyard. His interest in the yard he left to his son along with another of his most prized possessions, his copy of Mungo Murray's shipbuilding handbook, in which were written certain family records. This book, an early shipbuilder's bible published in 1756, had belonged to his grandfather. It was therefore being passed to the fourth generation of Marsh shipwrights.

Shipbuilding was still a sizeable business in Charleston in the last of the ante-bellum years. However, the age of commercial sail was past. Most of the vessels being built were steamships such as the 298-ton *Darlington* constructed in 1849 and the *Marion* built the next year. During the Civil War, Charleston builders were concerned, not with sailing vessels with "hearts of oak," but steamers with sides of iron.

A Charleston Man-Of-War [1]

It was the biggest event in Charleston since President George Washington had visited the city eight years before. "An immense crowd of citizens" came "by land and by water" early on a June morning in 1799 to watch the new frigate *John Adams* slide down the ways into the still waters of Shipyard Creek. The launching started and the vessel "moved with great velocity toward the water." Then she shuddered to a stop as the building ways settled in the soft ground.

Two days later, on the fifth of June, the anxious shipbuilders tried again. This time "she hurried from off her ways before a number of shores and blocks could be knocked away, and while a number of workmen (nine it is said) were still under her." The workmen survived as did the frigate which was on her way to a long and illustrious career with the new United States Navy.

The *John Adams* was built at Robert Cochran's small shipyard on Charleston Neck three miles above the city. Gathered there for her launching were many of the state's most prominent citizens. Among them were Governor Edward Rutledge and two of Charleston's heroes of the Revolution: Major General Charles Cotesworth Pinckney and Brigadier General William Washington.

It was a grand and festive occasion. The Madeira flowed freely as toast after toast was drunk in celebration.

As it turned out, the difficulty with the launching might better have been taken as a bad omen. For in a noble patriotic gesture, *John Adams* had been built and paid for by the people of Charleston as a gift to the United States Navy. She had an extraordinary career which took her all over the world — from the embattled harbor at Tripoli to the Fiji Islands to the South China Sea. Then in 1865 during the closing months of the Civil War, she returned to the place of her birth as a bitter enemy — as flagship of the inner blockading fleet of the Union Navy.

The story of the *John Adams* began, as have many great projects of Charlestonians, in a local tavern.

A MEETING IN WILLIAM'S LONG ROOM

In the 1790s Charleston was still the fourth largest city in the United States. While she retained much of her pre-Revolutionary elegance, and an immense civic and national pride, she was also, as always, a sailors' town. In 1793, Charleston became the main operating base in America for a considerable fleet of French privateers. Rowdy privateersmen swaggering down the streets with long sabers at their sides were a common sight. By 1798, however, Charlestonians, like other Americans, had grown disillusioned with the excesses of the French Republic, and the city, in common with the rest of the United States, was preparing for war with France. Fort Mechanic was built on what's now known as The Battery and Fort Pinckney was constructed on nearby Shutes Folly Island. And, on 30 June 1798, a meeting was held in William's Long Room to raise money to build a warship of twenty guns.

A citizens' committee was set up under the leadership of William Crafts. Many prominent residents became members, including Adam Gilchrist, Thomas Morris, David Alexander, Robert Hazlehurst, Adam Tunno, and James Miller. Within a month $100,000 had been raised for the vessel.

With this much money available, the committee decided to construct a larger warship. On 13 August its decision was announced: "it was resolved to build and equip a vessel of war of not less burthen than 550 tons, to carry 24 guns on the main deck." A committee of five was appointed "to carry into effect the subscribers' views." Its members were Crafts, Morris and Tunno of the original fund-raising group, who were joined by Henry Laurens, Jr. and Nathaniel Russell. (Russell, a new Englander known locally as "King of the Yankees," later built a splendid Adam-style mansion on Meeting Street that today is one of Charleston's pride and joys.)

Because of the manner by which she was paid for, the *John Adams* was known as a "subscription frigate." This financial arrangement was made under an Act of Congress passed on 30 June 1798, by coincidence the very same day that the Charleston group met at William's Long Room.

Four other American cities had also raised money to construct frigates for the Navy. The *Philadelphia*, the largest of the vessels, was built for the citizens of that city. The others were the *Essex*, the *Boston*, and the *New York*. Of these five ships, only *John Adams* would have a long career with the Navy. The *Philadelphia*, captured by the Barbary pirates, would be burned in Tripoli Harbor in 1804 in the famous raid led by Stephen Decatur, Jr. The *Boston* and the *New York* would be burned during the War of 1812 and the other frigate *Essex* captured by the British in 1814.

BUILDING THE SHIP

The Navy Department's plans for the *John Adams* were drafted by Assistant Naval Constructor Josiah Fox, a brilliant young naval architect who had worked

---

[1] This account of the Charleston-built frigate *John Adams* is a revised version of the similar piece in the first edition. Changes were made based on information developed during extensive research on the ship by W. M. P. Dunne of Hampton Days, N. Y. who also made a number of suggestions which improved the piece.

with Joshua Humphreys on the design of the *Constitution* and other new American frigates. The design was altered, however, by her master builder, Paul Pritchard, Jr., whose father had been in charge of the State Navy Yard at Hobcaw during the Revolution. Pritchard's changes included an increase in length of some five feet. James Marsh, Pritchard's foreman, and later a successful shipbuilder himself, oversaw the construction work. The *John Adams'* figurehead, a bust of President Adams, was sculpted by William Rush of Philadelphia, America's leading ship-carver, and local artisans completed her other carvings.

More than thirty shipwrights were brought in from Boston and Newburyport, Massachusetts to help build the frigate. By 10 November, the day her keel was laid, all the materials were ready at the yard. A local newspaper reported that "full 100 carpenters" would commence working on the vessel that week. Also at the yard by this time was Captain George Cross, USN, who would serve as the Navy's construction superintendent for the frigate and as her first commanding officer.

Cross was a well-known Charleston sea captain and merchant who had commanded an American privateer during the Revolution. How he came to be assigned to the *John Adams* is an intriguing story — one which involved the disgrace of the man who otherwise would have commanded the new vessel, Robert Cochran.

A native of New Hampshire, Cochran had long been Charleston's favorite sea captain. In May of 1791, he had served as coxswain of George Washington's ceremonial barge when it was rowed across the Cooper by twelve sea captains during the President's visit to the city. Cross served as one of the oarsmen.

With a direct appointment from President Washington, Cochran commanded a series of revenue cutters operating out of Charleston, beginning in 1793. In August of 1798 he was captain of the *Unanimity*, a 14-gun revenue schooner, cruising just north of Charleston near the Isle of Palms when he encountered a strange vessel. Although the vessel, an armed sloop, had hoisted British colors Cochran believed it to be a French privateer which had been lurking off the coast. The strange vessel fired a shot across *Unanimity's* bow and the vessels exchanged broadsides, each doing little damage. Despite the fact that his schooner was more heavily armed, Cochran fled to the safety of Dewees Inlet where the other deeper-draft vessel could not follow, eventually running *Unanimity* aground.

The next day, the strange vessel put into Charleston. It turned out to be the British sloop-of-war *Mosquito*. The captain lodged a complaint over the incident with the British consul, accusing Cochran of cowardice. It turned out that each vessel had mistaken the other for the French privateer. The naval protocol of the times would have required Cochran to sail his vessel within hailing distance of the other and use his speaking trumpet to identify himself. His failure to

"speak *Mosquito*," and the fact that he fled before the inferior vessel, were considered by the Navy to be improper conduct and as a consequence Cochran fell into disgrace.

At the time of the incident, the naval brig *General Pinckney* was being fitted out in Charleston, with Cochran as prospective commanding officer. As a result of the *Unanimity* incident, South Carolina Congressmen Robert Goodlow Harper and John Rutledge, Jr. proposed that George Cross be appointed as captain instead of Cochran. Shortly thereafter, the Secretary of the Navy obtained the approval of President Adams and Cross was commissioned a captain in the Navy on 10 September 1798.

Cross was first given command of *Unanimity*. Then he was transferred to the *General Pinckney*. Cross's command of *General Pinckney* also was short lived. On 31 October 1798, Secretary of the Navy Benjamin Stoddert ordered him to relinquish his command of the brig and appointed him commanding officer of *John Adams* as construction of the frigate was beginning at the shipyard on Charleston Neck.

As the November days grew shorter and fitting out of Pritchard's new revenue schooner *South Carolina* got underway at the shipyard on Charleston Neck, construction work on the *John Adams* began in earnest. The frigate was built of the finest shipbuilding woods available: Carolina live oak, cedar and long leaf pine.

The ship's frames, constructed of curved sections called futtocks, were made of live oak except for the top timbers which were Lowcountry cedar. Her keel was fashioned from pine as was her keelson, the longitudinal member on the inside of the ship just above the keel. Carefully selected knot-free, long leaf pine timbers, also from local forests, were used for the masts and spars. Her deck beams were cut from yellow pine logs hewn along the Edisto River south of Charleston. The knees used to support the deck were made of live oak.

Shipbuilding practices of that time required much hard work, best done in Charleston in the cooler months. Vessels were built in the open, exposed to the weather to season the oak used for the frames and other structural members of the hull. The long pine logs were stored underwater in a spar pond at the yard to keep them sound and resilient. The timbers were cut by sawyers over a saw pit and shaped using broadaxe and adz. They were then joined together with wooden pegs called treenails, pounded in holes bored into the wood by use of augers. Heavy timbers (those over four inches thick were known as "thick stuff") were joined by bolts of iron or copper. The seams were caulked with tons of oakum, tarred rope fibers, pounded in with mallets. Pitch, heated in huge kettles, was used to cover the caulked seams and then the entire hull was planed smooth. Copper sheathing was nailed to the hull below the waterline to protect it from shipworms and to reduce the accumulation of barnacles and other marine growth. In Charleston, much of this work was done by slaves.

Following her launching in June of 1799, *John Adams* was moved three miles down the Cooper to Gadsden's wharf, which was located at what is now the foot of Calhoun Street. Here the fitting-out of the vessel was begun.

At Gadsden's Wharf, the three lower masts of *John Adams* were put in place. Miles of rope went into her rigging, the stays and shrouds supporting the masts and yards and the network of running rigging to work the sails.

The vessel was returned to Pritchard's yard for additional work. Then on 16 July Captain Cross brought her back to the city as other vessels along the way lowered their colors in her honor. The new frigate was anchored off Prioleau's Wharf at the foot of Queen Street, where the President's boat had landed in May of 1791. Here she was greeted by "federal huzzahs" of seamen on nearby vessels and from cheering citizens standing on the shore.

The next day Captain Cross began the difficult task of recruiting the 220 men required to make up the crew. A local newspaper reported that a rendezvous was being established at "the south east corner of the Governor's Bridge on East Bay for enlisting a crew of brave tars." (This bridge, a wide brick arch, spanned the creek that was filled in to build the Market a few years later.) Able seamen were not easy to enlist in Charleston and several months later the Secretary of the Navy expressed concern as to whether Cross could raise an adequate crew. Despite the secretary's misgivings, he was able to recruit enough men from the local area to sail and fight his proud ship.

She was, indeed, the most powerful warship that had ever been built in Charleston. The battery of the frigate consisted of twenty-six twelve-pounders and six twenty-four pound carronades. These cannons, from the naval stores at Philadelphia, had been brought to Charleston aboard the merchantman *South Carolina*. The *John Adams* became the first U. S. Navy vessel to include carronades, a short-barreled weapon throwing a heavy ball, as part of her original battery.

While anchored off Prioleau's Wharf, *John Adams* was prepared for sea. Her upper masts were installed and the final fitting-out completed. Stores were loaded, her water casks filled, and her crew assembled. Although his original orders were to sail to Cayenne, French Guiana, Captain Cross received in October a new directive from Secretary Stoddert to proceed to Puerto Rico. The frigate was to cruise in the vicinity for a month and then join the Guadeloupe Squadron under the command of Commodore Thomas Truxtun.

By 23 October, the new ship was ready for sea. She weighed anchor and sailed gracefully past the town firing "a grand salute" which was returned by the guns of Fort Mechanic. Because of a strong easterly breeze, she came to anchor south of the town off James Island to await a favorable wind before attempting the tricky passage across the bar.

CROSSING THE BAR

On 30 October the big day finally came. Cross weighed anchor and the *John Adams* surged past Fort Johnson, her guns booming a salute which the fort returned gun for gun. A short while later she crossed the bar and embarked on her maiden voyage, and a long and glorious career protecting America's interests around the world.

She was a fine vessel, "a very handsome ship, and, in all respects, does ample justice to the skill and abilities of Mr. Paul Pritchard, the master builder." Rated at 544 tons, she was known as the smallest of the five subscription frigates. The Charleston pilot, a Mr. Delano, who first took her out of the harbor said that she sailed "remarkably well." Cross himself pronounced her "in the 1st Class of sailers."

Ten years later Josiah Fox had an opportunity to closely examine the frigate and found that, "From an unknown cause she is wider on the Larboard than Starboard Side, and always tends to list to Starboard, from which circumstance I am inclined to believe she will be considerably stiffer on the Starboard than the Larboard Tack." None of her logs mention this tendency, however. In any case when she went into service in 1799 *John Adams* was an important addition to the Navy, for at that time there were only five ships in the fleet that carried more firepower than the Charleston frigate's 228 pound broadside.

After crossing the bar, *John Adams* sailed southward to Puerto Rico and joined the Leeward Squadron at St. Kitts. By September of 1800, she had captured the French privateers *Le Jason* and *Le Decade* and recaptured eight merchant vessels that had been taken by the French raiders. The rest of the year she spent in the West Indies protecting American shipping against the privateers of the French Republic.

By the winter of 1800, peace had been made with France. *John Adams* was ordered back to Charleston where Cross paid off the crew and arranged for the vessel to be repaired and reequipped for sea. Cross himself was placed on furlough and was discharged from the Navy in June of 1801. The first cruise of the *John Adams* had lasted 397 days, of which only thirty-five were spent in port, a unique record in the early Navy.

GLORY AT TRIPOLI

The frigate's next assignment was against a formidable foe — the pirates of the Barbary Coast. With a new Commanding Officer, Captain John Rodgers, she sailed for the Mediterranean from Hampton Road on 22 October 1802. *John Adams* operated with the American squadron stationed there until the next May when she was ordered to cruise independently off Tripoli. Upon arrival at the city, her guns pounded the fort and the gunboats anchored under its protection.

A short time later, the Charleston frigate captured the Tripolitan cruiser *Meshouda*, a notorious member of the pirate fleet. Then, reinforced by her sister subscription frigate *New York* and the schooner *Enterprise*, she chased a flotilla of enemy gunboats back into the harbor. On 21 June, *John Adams* and *Enterprise* captured a 22-gun pirate vessel in what was considered one of the most important victories of the war. In less than two months *John Adams* had defeated the two largest ships in the navy of the Pasha of Tripoli.

The *John Adams* continued operations in the Mediterranean under Hugh G. Campbell of Charleston and then made two cruises as a storeship under Isaac Chauncey and John Shaw. On 29 November 1805 she returned to the Washington Navy Yard for conversion to a corvette, which mainly involved a reduction in armament as these vessels were intended to serve primarily as commerce raiders. Upon completion, she cruised off our coast from May 1809 to December 1811 under Samuel Evans and Joseph Tarbell.

When the War of 1812 began, the *John Adams* was in Boston being altered, yet again, the changes including mounting eighteen-pounder carronades on her quarterdeck. Charles Ludlow assumed command in July and took her to New York City where she stayed until 1814, when she departed from there under a flag-of-truce, carrying the peace commissioners Henry Clay and Jonathan Russell to Sweden. She was joined at Gothenburg by a third commissioner, John Quincy Adams, after whose father the frigate had been named.

The autumn of 1815 saw the veteran frigate back in the Mediterranean, where she arrived too late to participate in Commodore Decatur's victory over the Algerian pirates. The next year *John Adams* returned to America to do battle with pirates much closer to home who were infesting the West Indies. In December 1817 she was the flagship of the American squadron that captured Amelia Island in Spanish East Florida, the base of the notorious buccaneer, Commodore Aury.

Five years after her voyage with the peace envoys, the Charleston man-of-war undertook another diplomatic mission, serving as the flagship of Commodore Oliver Hazard Perry. Perry, hero of the Battle of Lake Erie in the War of 1812, was asked to negotiate with Venezuela for the protection American merchant ships against the privateers who plagued the waters off the Spanish Main. On 7 June 1819 the *John Adams* departed from Annapolis for Angostura, Venezuela (now Ciudad Bolívar) 300 miles up the Orinoco River. Perry's mission was successful but he was stricken with yellow fever coming downriver and died before rejoining his flagship.

The *John Adams* was in the Mediterranean again in 1820 and from there she was ordered to the West Africa squadron and took part in the capture of four slave ships. She joined the West India Squadron in 1823 as the flagship of Commodore David Porter.

By 1825, the Charleston man-of-war had seen a quarter century of service in the U. S. Navy. She had fought pirates from the Caribbean Sea to the Gulf of Sidra and sailed in harms way on many occasions. Then in November of 1825 disaster struck when she was on a peaceful mission, a survey of Pensacola harbor which was to be used as home port for the West India Squadron.

As she was sailing into the harbor, she was driven onto the bar by adverse winds and current. On board were three of the Navy's top brass: Commodores William Bainbridge, Lewis Warrington and James Biddle. In Biddle's words, "Never before was a ship that escaped so near to going to Davy Jones."

REINCARNATION AT NORFOLK

In 1829, the old *John Adams* died. The following year she was reincarnated at the Norfolk Navy Yard in an an administrative sleight-of-hand.

In May of 1803, the guns of the Charleston-built frigate John Adams *pounded the fortified city of Tripoli and the pirate gunboats in the harbor.* John Adams, *built at the shipyard on Charleston Neck in 1798 and 1799, was paid for by the people of Charleston and turned over to the United States Navy as a patriotic gift.*

Drawing by Charles Mulligan.

The Charleston frigate's last voyage was into Hampton Roads where she was to be rebuilt at the Norfolk Navy Yard (then known as the Gosport Navy Yard). According to Howard Chapelle, the noted historian of naval architecture, it was found that many of her timbers had rotted to the point where rebuilding wasn't practical. Rather than reconstruct the old vessel to the original design, funds for the rebuilding were used to build a new ship, retaining the identity of the original. The reincarnated *John Adams* was built as a 24-gun corvette or sloop-of-war, becoming one of a series of similar vessels designed by Samuel Humphreys, whose father had designed the *Constitution*. *John Adams* was now about 127'6" long on the gundeck with a beam of approximately 33'9". The original main timbers were retained in the conversion along with the tradition of three decades of faithful service in protecting the interests of the new republic.

The rebuilt *John Adams* sailed to the Mediterranean in 1831 carrying her old commander David Porter to his post as U. S. minister to the Ottoman Empire. In 1833, *John Adams* operated off the Turkish coast before returning to the United States on a voyage which took her to Morocco, Liberia and the West Indies. For the next three years she served once again in the Mediterranean. Following a refit at New York City, she and the frigate *Columbia* made an around-the-world cruise showing the flag for the United States.

When the *John Adams* and her squadron arrived at Columbo, Ceylon they received word that the American ship *Eclipse* had been attacked by natives at Soo-Soo, Sumatra. The squadron immediately sailed to the scene of the incident. Upon arrival the American warships bombarded the forts at Quallah Battoo and two other cities in retaliation.

In 1842 the *John Adams* joined the Brazil Squadron for three years, returning to New York in late 1844. Early the next year she was ordered to join the Home Squadron in the Gulf of Mexico for operations in the Mexican War from 1845 through 1848. The following five years of her career were spent in action with the British Navy against slavers off West Africa and conducting a hydrographic survey of the African coast. During this period she carried the survivors of the ship-sloop *Yorktown* back to America. *Yorktown*, the first American warship to bear this name, had struck an uncharted reef in the Cape Verde Islands while cruising against slavers off the African coast.

A LESSON FOR THE CANNIBALS

John Adam's next mission in 1855 was perhaps the most unusual of the Charleston ship's long career. She sailed across the Pacific to the Fiji Islands where native cannibals were making a habit of eating American seaman. There the *John Adams* bombarded five Fijian towns to show the islanders that the U. S. Navy didn't take such acts lightly.

The next year found *John Adams* anchored off San Francisco to help put down a vigilante insurrection there. Not long afterwards she was off to the China Station where she took part in the defense of Canton during the Taiping Rebellion of 1860.

Upon her return to America, the old warhorse was put out to pasture. This took the form of an assignment to the Naval Academy, at its Civil War home at Newport, Rhode Island. Here, she along with the sloops-of-war *Macedonian* and *Marion* was used to train midshipmen to sail. But as it turned out, her career as a warship wasn't quite over.

AN IRONIC HOMECOMING

In August of 1863, she sailed to Port Royal, South Carolina to join the South Atlantic Blockading Squadron. There she remained for several months as a storeship until late December when she joined the inner blockading fleet at Charleston.

By the time *John Adams* arrived, Fort Sumter had been reduced to a pile of smoking rubble and long-range Federal guns on Morris Island were relentlessly pounding the beleagured city. The initially-porous blockade of Charleston had tightened. The powerful blockading fleet was divided into an inner fleet inside the bar and an outer ring of vessels. Blockade runners in their low-silhouetted Clyde-built steamers dared make the run only on moonless nights; daylight attempts were a thing of the past.

When *John Adams* took up station off Morris Island around Christmastime in 1863, there were sixteen other vessels inside the bar, including the fearsome *New Ironsides*, and nine more in the outer fleet. Many of the ships were ironclad steamers and steam-powered sloops-of-war, powerful vessels, but not invulnerable to attack. On 22 February 1864, *John Adams* took aboard forty survivors of the sloop-of-war *Housatonic*, which had been sunk by the Confederate submarine *H. L. Hunley*. The *Housatonic* thereby gained the dubious distinction of being the first warship ever sunk by a submarine in naval warfare.

During the first week of July 1864 the *John Adams* captured the blockade runner *Pocahontas*. On 24 July 1864, she became the flagship of Captain J. F. Green, then senior officer in charge of the inner fleet. At this time, armed with heavy Dahlgren guns and Parrott rifles as well as smaller cannons, she served as both munitions store-ship and flagship of the Federal vessels.

She remained at this post until February of 1865 when the Confederate forces evacuated Charleston before the advance of Sherman's armies. Then she sailed into the harbor and into the Cooper River where the original vessel had been built by the people of Charleston sixty-six years before. This time there were no "federal huzzahs" by cheering citizens standing on the shore.

A POSTSCRIPT

To the men who sailed them, the old wooden warships were much more than just a structure of planks and timbers, propelled by sheets of cloth that caught the wind. They were home — however cramped and dark and damp — for months and sometimes years on end. They were a haven in battle, although hardly safe with flying balls and splinters, blinding smoke and the deafening boom of cannons. To their countries, they were powerful instruments of national policy which could extend a nation's influence anywhere the ships could sail.

The figurehead on the prow was a visible symbol of the belief that they embodied human qualities. If ships truly were alive, as some old-time sailors believed, what tales the Charleston man-of-war could have told.

The old *John Adams* ended her Navy service in Boston where she was sold in October of 1867. Her builders were long dead. Pritchard had died in 1815, while still building ships at his Fairbank shipyard on Daniel's Island, across the Wando River from his father's old State Navy Yard at Hobcaw. Robert Cochran, who owned the shipyard where the frigate was built, was dismissed from the Revenue Service (the modern day Coast Guard) because of the *Unanimity* incident. He died in 1824 at the age of eighty-eight and was buried in a family cemetery near the site of his old shipyard. Captain Cross died in 1816 and was buried at St. Michael's graveyard in Charleston, as was James Marsh who was a wealthy man when he died at the age of eighty.

When James Marsh was laid to rest, the *John Adams* had seen more than a half-century of naval service and was patroling the coast of Africa against the slave traffic. It is doubtful whether Marsh, or any other of the frigate's builders, knew the full measure of their ship's accomplishments during his own lifetime. Memories of the Charleston man-of-war will never die, however, as long as there is a U. S. Navy.

The John Adams *in the Mediterranean in 1837.*

The 313-ton steamer Planter was built at Charleston in 1860. She served as a transport and an armed dispatch boat early in the war. At four o'clock in the morning on 12 May 1862, she was stolen by her pilot, Robert Smalls, a Negro slave. While the captain was ashore, Smalls boldly sailed her past the harbor forts and turned her over to a vessel of the Union blockading fleet.

Typical of Confederate blockade runners was the Robert E. Lee, a low-slung Clyde-built steamer. The 900-ton vessel could make 13.5 knots. On 28 December 1862, she arrived off Charleston bar on her first voyage from Nassau, laden with goods for the Confederacy. However, the local pilot refused to take her past the blockade. She steamed north to Wilmington where she established a nearly legendary reputation as an elusive blockade runner. Her Wilmington pilot, Archibald Gutherie, was the author's great-great grandfather.

Naval Historical Center photo of painting at the Museum of the Confederacy, Richmond, Va.

The Chicora and the Palmetto State, two big Confederate ironclad rams, lie serenely in Charleston Harbor in this Conrad Wise Chapman painting. Both were built in Charleston in 1862, the Chicora by James M. Eason, her sistership by Cameron and company. Shortly before dawn on 31 January 1863, they crept into the inner blockading fleet and disabled two Federal vessels before steaming back to the safety of the harbor. Both ironclads were destroyed by Confederate forces when Charleston fell in February of 1865.

Naval Historical Center photo from *Harper's Weekly*, 1861.

The steamer Marion, built at Charleston in 1850, was used to lay obstructions in the harbor early in the Civil War. On the night of 6 April 1863, she sank in the Ashley River after drifting loose from her moorings.

David and Goliath

One of the most remarkable naval vessels in American history was a product of the ingenuity of Charlestonians faced with a fearsome enemy — the huge ironclad Union warship *New Ironsides*.

Little David was the vessel's name, chosen to signify her purpose — to combat the mighty Goliath lurking just outside of Charleston Harbor. Her creators were as diverse a group imaginable. She was designed by a Charleston physician, who was also a notable agricultural chemist. She was built by a transplanted Marylander who had been in the lumber business before the war. Her spar torpedo armament was designed by a leading Charleston architect.

Little David was built in a shed at a Cooper River rice plantation, Stoney Point, which was owned by her designer, Dr. St. Julien Ravenel. Her hull was fashioned from an old boiler into a new and bold shape — like a long, thin, sharp-pointed cigar. Her steam engine was taken from an old locomotive. Francis D. Lee, better known for his fine Victorian houses, designed an explosive charge mounted on the end of a long spar attached to her bow. In charge of the construction as head mechanic was David Ebaugh. Most of the workmen were Negro plantation hands. The project was financed by Charlestonian Theodore D. Stoney, who saw in *New Ironsides* the power to utterly destroy the defenses of his beloved city.

Construction of the strange vessel proceeded in great secrecy at Stoney Point in the fall of 1863. Finally she was ready. The plantation hands loaded her on a flatcar and the vessel was taken by train to Atlantic Wharf in downtown Charleston. Here she was lowered into the muddy waters of the Cooper River. She floated so that only a few inches of her hull and her small funnel were visible above the water, just as Dr. Ravenel had planned.

By this time the city was under siege by long-range guns of the Union stronghold on Morris Island. Battery Wagner on Morris Island had been abandoned. Fort Sumter lay in ruins. It was time to act.

Theodore Stoney showed *Little David* to a Confederate naval officer, a Virginia lieutenant named W. T. Glassell. Glassell, who was impressed with Lee's invention of the spar torpedo, enthusiastically agreed to command the sleek little vessel. From other Confederate naval craft in the harbor he chose three volunteers for a crew: James Tomb as engineer, James Sullivan as fireman, and J. Walker Cannon as pilot.

At dusk on 5 October 1863, *Little David* ventured into the harbor, her low shape barely visible above the waves. She passed Fort Sumter and crept unseen among the vessels of the inner fleet in search of the dreaded *New Ironsides*. As she approached the huge vessel she was hailed by a sentry. Glassell made no answer, cocking a double-barrelled shotgun, which he had brought along so he would be able to fire the first shot. Then the officer of the deck called out, "What boat is that?". With *Little David* about forty yards from the Goliath, Glassell fired both barrels, fatally wounding the Federal officer. A few seconds later the torpedo struck *New Ironsides* and exploded, shaking her from stem to stern.

Water poured in *Little David*'s funnel, dousing her boiler fire. Aboard *New Ironsides* the drummer beat to quarters and men scurried to their battle stations. Meanwhile on *Little David*, Glassell ordered his crew to abandon ship, diving in the water himself amid a hail of small arms fire.

Cannon the pilot, who couldn't swim, stayed aboard. A few minutes later *Little David* drifted away from the bigger vessel and James Tomb clambered back aboard with Cannon. The two of them managed to get the boiler fired up and, amazingly, made it back to Charleston with their little torpedo boat intact. Glassell and Sullivan were picked up later by Union vessels and taken prisoner.

The *New Ironsides* had sustained considerable damage. She remained on station, however, until May of 1864 when she steamed to Philadelphia for repairs.

Little David, conceived by a physician-chemist, built by a lumberman, armed by an architect, and paid for by a Charlestonian to protect his beloved city, had mounted the first successful torpedo attack on a warship in naval history.

The awesome ironclad steamer New Ironsides arrived at Charleston on 17 January 1863 to join the blockading fleet as Admiral Dupont's flagship. Mounting fourteen eleven-inch guns and two huge 150-pound Parrott rifles, she was probably the most powerful warship of her era — a true Goliath.

Smithsonian Institution photograph courtesy Naval Historical Center.

This full-scale model of the Little David is located at Moncks Corner, South Carolina, not far from the site of the old plantation where the little spar torpedo boat was built. On 5 October 1863, Little David attacked the New Ironsides just outside of Charleston Harbor, heavily damaging the huge Federal ironclad steamer.

Photo by Palmer Olliff.

29

Palmer Olliff photograph of model at the Charleston Museum.

In the bright moonlit night of 17 February 1864, the Confederate submarine H. L. Hunley met her destiny two miles off the Isle of Palms. She sank the Federal steam sloop-of-war Housatonic using a "Lee spar-torpedo" like that of Little David. It would be more than half a century before another submarine would sink a warship in combat.

A number of similar vessels were built at Charleston after the success of the original Little David. Like beached whales, the spar torpedo boats littered the shores of Charleston Harbor after the end of the war.

PLAN

SHOWING PROPOSED GENERAL DEVELOPMENT

U.S. NAVAL STATION

CHARLESTON S C

Reduced from Blue Print furnished by U S Navy Department,
in City Surveyors Office Charleston SC

Scale of feet

2
The Greatest Naval Station At The South

On a hot summer afternoon in 1901, a child was born in the cottage of the keeper of the park at Chicora.

The mother, a strong-willed but sometimes fickle lass, had lived at Port Royal for many years. The father had wooed her to Charleston with promises of a fine home. His city had welcomed her with open arms. A few years later, the father had gone but the mother and her child had a lovely place to live beside the Cooper River.

At first the mother was uncomfortable with her offspring. She blamed its godfather, claiming that the child was his and saying that she never really wanted it. But as the years passed the child grew strong with the godfather's help, and eventually the mother accepted it as her own.

The child, of course, was the Navy Yard. If the Navy Department was its mother, its father was the genteel Mayor of Charleston, J. Adger Smyth. And its godfather, who helped with the birth and looked after it as it grew up, was a man as unlike the father as night from day — Benjamin Ryan Tillman.

The Navy Yard at Charleston had been made possible by improvements to the harbor, designed and carried out by the Army Corps of Engineers. By the turn of the century, the channel was nearly twice as deep as it had been two decades before. The yard was established on the west bank of the Cooper River, a mile to the north of where the old shipyard on Charleston Neck once stood.

In the spring of 1902 construction of the shipyard began. The most important facility was the dry dock, which took five years to complete. By 1909, five shop buildings and the power house had been built and the new dry dock was in operation.

The work of repairing ships had begun at the yard well before the original facilities were completed. By 1909, there were 300 civilian workmen at the yard and about a score of naval officers. In the following years, the workload increased and the yard grew and diversified, developing a characteristic versatility that would become its hallmark.

In 1912, a Navy machinist mates school was started. The following year, the first vessels were built by the yard, two paddle-wheel steamboats for the Corps of Engineers. In 1914, a naval clothing factory was set up that eventually employed 1,000 women. The yard built a ferryboat and a tug that towed it to Rhode Island.

As the war in Europe raged, work at the Navy Yard increased. By the time the United States entered the First World War in April of 1917, there were approximately 1,700 employees at the yard. Among them was an old man in the Boiler Shop whose experience went back to the days of the Confederate Navy. His name was John K. McKenzie and he had once worked on the submarine *H. L. Hunley*. ⚓

The original development plan for "the greatest naval station at the South" called for two dry docks; it would be more than forty years before the second one was built. Near the bottom of the map, on the west side of Shipyard Creek, was the location of the old shipyard where Paul Pritchard, Jr. built the frigate John Adams *in 1799.*

Quincey Gillmore and His Jetties

It is one of the ironies of Charleston history that Quincey Gillmore, who had directed the Union bombardment of the city and her forts during the Civil War, would also develop the improvements to the harbor that opened the port to the deep-draft vessels of the twentieth century and made possible the establishment of the Navy Yard.

Gillmore, as a colonel in the Military Engineers, had been a member of a commission that had surveyed the harbor for potential improvements before the start of the Civil War. The war took its toll on Charleston's splendid harbor; first

the sunken whalers of the Stone Fleet blocked the main shipping channel, and by the war's end the channels were littered with shipwrecks.

In 1869, Colonel Gillmore was placed in charge of coastal defenses from Cape Fear to St. Augustine and in the following year became the supervising engineer for surveys of rivers and harbors in that region. The first step taken at Charleston was to clear the channel of wrecks. This was done over the next few years. The many shipwrecks removed included those of the *Palmetto State*, the *Charleston* and the *Chicora*, all Charleston-built Confederate ironclads destroyed

At his headquarters on Morris Island, Brigadier General Quincey Gillmore studies his map and plots the destruction of Charleston and her forts. His long range guns, such as the dreaded Swamp Angel, could hurl exploding shells more than four miles to the city. By the fall of 1863, they had reduced the walls of Fort Sumter to piles of rubble.

to prevent their falling into Yankee hands. Also removed were the wrecks of the Federal ironclad monitors *Weehawken* and *Patapsco* and the sloop-of-war *Housatonic*, which had been sunk by the Confederate submarine *H. L. Hunley.*

The channels at the mouth of the harbor were now clear of wrecks but they had never been more than about twelve feet deep at low water — too shallow for the larger vessels then going into service. In 1876, Gillmore had a survey made of the harbor and then developed a plan for improvements. The next year he and the two United States senators from South Carolina, M. C. Butler and "Honest John" Patterson, went to Washington and convinced the Congress to appropriate $200,000 to carry out his plan.

Gillmore's plan was simple in concept. It involved constructing two converging jetties to channel the power of the ebb tide to maintain a new twenty-one-foot-deep channel. A major engineering problem was to design the jetties to obtain precisely the right amount of tidal flow. Portions of the jetties were designed to be below the surface to allow the tide to come in normally and still keep the channel clear of mud. The exact height of the jetties would be determined later.

Construction began immediately. Platforms, or "mattresses" as they were called, were fashioned of logs and covered with brush. These were towed into place between two barges loaded with "one-man" stones. Thirty to sixty tons of the stone were placed on each platform, which then settled on the bottom to form a portion of the foundation for the jetties.

Courtesy U. S. Miltary Academy.

In 1876, Quincey Gillmore, then a colonel in the Military Engineers, designed the improvements to Charleston Harbor that opened the port to deep-draft vessels of the twentieth century and made the Navy Yard possible.

Courtesy U. S. Military Academy.

Frederick V. Abbot came to Charleston in 1884 as a first lieutenant in the Corps of Engineers and directed the jetties project to its completion. In January of 1901, Abbot gave key testimony about conditions in the harbor in congressional hearings related to establishment of the Navy Yard.

Work continued on the jetties foundation for the next several years. It was finally completed in 1885, the year in which the new dredge *Charleston*, which Gillmore had built for the project, began clearing the channel. The jetties were finally finished a decade later under the direction of Frederick V. Abbot.

Abbot had arrived in Charleston in 1884 as a first lieutenant of engineers, five years out of West Point. He managed the project until its completion in 1895, establishing the final height of the portions of the jetties below the surface by careful flow measurements as the layers of stones were laid. By that time, the main shipping channel had been deepened to 17½ feet at mean low water. By 1900, continued dredging operations had produced a twenty-three-foot-deep channel. Thanks to Quincy Gillmore, Charleston entered the twentieth century with a first-class harbor, more than adequate for the site of a navy yard.

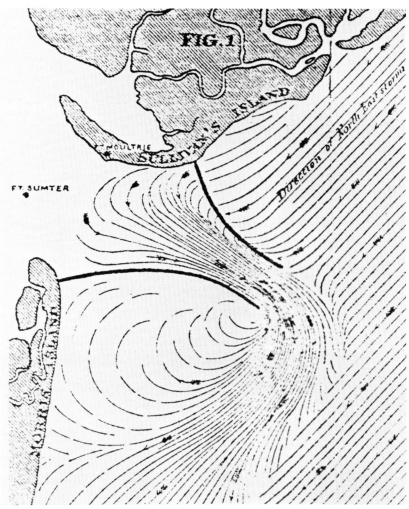

This sketch accompanied Gillmore's original plan to build jetties to improve Charleston Harbor.

This boat repair shop was built at Port Royal during the Civil War. The Navy maintained a presence here until after the turn of the century.

National Archives photograph, courtesy The Citadel Museum.

Early in the Civil War, the Federal Navy captured Port Royal Harbor and there established an operating base for the South Atlantic Blockading Squadron. This machine shop was built at St. Helens to support repairs to the fleet.

National Archives photograph, courtesy The Citadel Museum.

In 1896, the double-turreted monitor Amphitrite was repaired in the new dry dock at the Parris Island Naval Station at Port Royal. Before the turn of the century, the small wooden dock had become obsolete.

The Founding of the Navy Yard

In a way, the founding of the Navy Yard was similar to the settlement of the city. Like the first colonists, the Navy went to Port Royal and then was convinced to move on to Charleston. Both were persuaded to move by the leader of the people living at their destination.

In the Navy's case, the man involved was not an Indian chief who lived on the Ashley River but a white-haired gentleman who occupied the city hall on Broad Street. In his campaign to induce the Navy to move to Charleston, the mayor had a powerful ally — a crude, one-eyed farmer from Edgefield County who had become a member of the Naval Affairs Committee of the United States Senate.

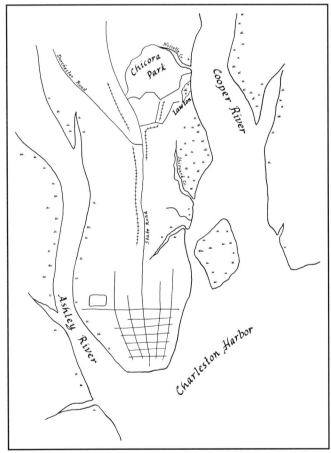

In 1901, the area north of Charleston was mostly forest with a few scattered farms and a number of fertilizer factories. The Chicora Park tract owned by the city contained nearly 600 acres.

In the first year of the Civil War, the Federal Navy captured Port Royal Harbor which became the operating base for the South Atlantic Blockading Squadron. After the war, the Navy maintained a small presence in the Port Royal area and eventually a naval station was built on Parris Island. In 1889, a Navy commission recommended Port Royal as the best place for a new navy yard between Norfolk and the Florida straits. In 1891, construction of a wooden dry dock on Parris Island was begun. The dock was completed four years later but was never satisfactory, for it was too small for larger warships and the wooden timbers became infested with shipworms. Moreover, by 1898 the Navy had decided to replace all its wooden dry docks with ones made of stone or concrete.

The following year Charlestonians, who had been closely watching the developments at Port Royal, decided to move. Mayor J. Adger Smyth journeyed to Washington to meet with South Carolina Senator Benjamin Ryan Tillman and enlist his support in moving the Parris Island Naval Station to Charleston. They must have formed a curious pair, the genteel mayor of Charleston and "Pitchfork Ben" Tillman.

Tillman had served four years as governor of South Carolina beginning in 1892, during which time he started Clemson College and harassed hard-drinking Charlestonians with laws banning liquor sales in the state. He got his nickname from an 1896 U. S. Senate campaign speech in which he avowed, if elected, to stick a pitchfork in President Cleveland, right, "in his old fat ribs." Tillman won the election and soon afterwards became a member of the Naval Affairs Committee. He never got to stick his pitchfork in the President. He did, however, help bring the Navy Yard to Charleston and in the early years did more than anyone to keep it there.

Armed with facts about improvements to the harbor and other advantages Charleston offered, Mayor Smyth convinced Tillman to take up the city's cause. The two of them met with Admiral Endicott, Chief of the Bureau of Yards and Docks, and other Navy officials to present Charleston's case. On 29 June 1900, the Secretary of the Navy appointed a board of naval officers to determine whether the Parris Island Naval Station should be moved to Charleston. After visiting both sites and hearing lengthy arguments by each side, the board recommended the Chicora Park site at Charleston.

Charleston leaders wanted the navy yard badly, to help rejuvenate a poor economy that had never fully recovered from the Civil War. A measure of the importance of the yard to the city was the offer of the Chicora Park site. On the Cooper River where the old Turnbull Place was located, the city was developing a magnificent recreational park. It had been designed by the well-known Massachusetts firm of Olmsted Brothers, who had created the beautiful gardens at Biltmore House in Asheville a few years before. It was an ambitious project with salt water lagoons and landscaped gardens. By the turn of the century, a wharf and service buildings had been constructed, a nursery established, the lagoons and bridges built and golf links laid out. The Turnbull Plantation house was being turned into an inn. A pavilion had been built and many Charlestonians took the trolley to the park to picnic and dance on summer evenings.

The city had arranged for the Navy to purchase the property to the south as well. Adjacent to Chicora Park was the site of the old Marshlands Plantation, then known as the Lawton Place. To the south of it and extending to Shipyard Creek were 760 acres, mostly marshlands, which were owned by the city, having previously been obtained from the state.

Library of Congress.

The genteel demeanor of this formal portrait was hardly the image that Benjamin Ryan Tillman, United States Senator from South Carolina, presented to his opponents. As a powerful member of the Naval Affairs Committee, Tillman helped bring the Navy Yard to Charleston and did more than anyone to keep it there in the early years. Many called it his navy yard in the beginning. "Pitchfork Ben," the delight of political cartoonists, was a down-to-earth farmer from Edgefield County who as governor was perhaps best known for his efforts to sober-up Charleston and for starting Clemson College.

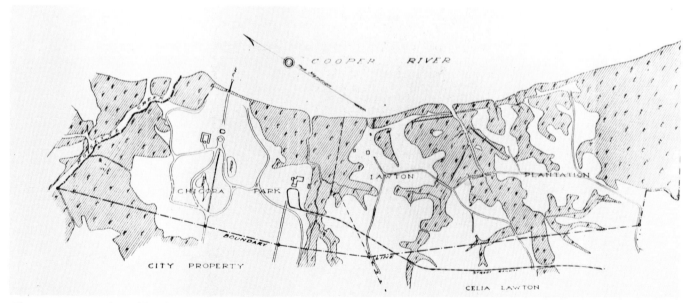

The property purchased by the navy included 171 acres of Chicora Park, 258 acres of the Lawton Place, and 760 acres of marshland to the south. It is obvious from this plan why the old plantation then known as the Lawton Place had been called Marshlands.

On 12 August 1901, the Navy took possession of the property. Captain Edwin Longnecker, who represented the Navy, had arrived in Charleston from Washington the day before, accompanied by the government paymaster, Major Skelding. On the afternoon of the twelfth, they took the trolley to the site and made a final inspection of the property. Once this was done, a check in the amount of $34,307 was given to the city for 171 acres of Chicora Park and one for $50,000 to Mrs. Celia Lawton's representative for 258 acres of the old Marshlands Plantation. The city conveyed the 760 acres of marshland to the south to the Navy for one dollar.

The ceremony of "taking formal possession" took place "at the pretty little cottage of the keeper of the park at Chicora." After the formalities were completed, Captain Longnecker and Major Skelding and the Charleston party led by Mayor Smyth were served a "light luncheon" and drank a number of toasts to celebrate the occasion. Longnecker, who would become the first commandant of the new yard, stated that he was "delighted with the look of the land" and said that the Navy Department had "acted most wisely in selecting Charleston for the greatest naval station at the South."

After obtaining the property, the Navy lost little time in getting started. The plans for the dry dock had already been approved and in a few weeks bids were being solicited for its construction.

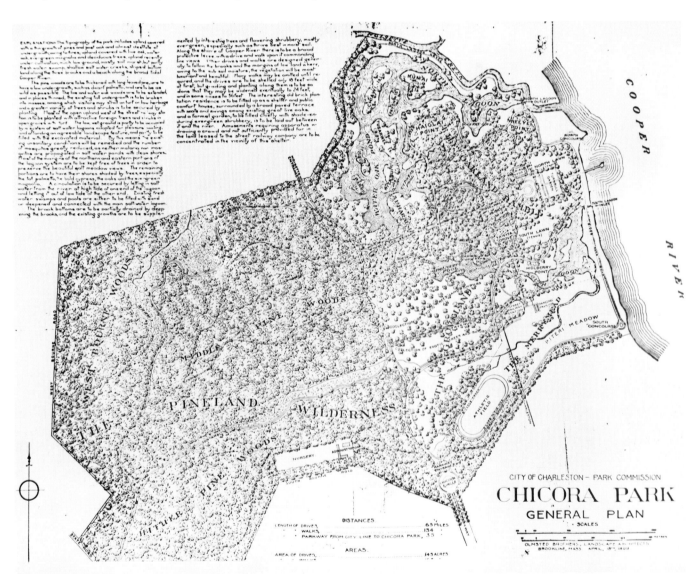

City of Charleston Yearbook — 1900.

Chicora Park was an ambitious development for the city of Charleston. The beautiful park was a popular place for picnics and dancing at the pavilion on summer evenings. That the city gave up the park was a measure of just how important it was to Charleston's leaders for the city to become home of the new navy yard.

On 12 August 1901, Captain Edwin Longnecker took possession of the site of the yard for the Navy. Longnecker also served as the first commandant.

It was in this house, "the pretty little cottage of the keeper of the park at Chicora," that Captain Longnecker took formal possession of the site of the yard for the U. S. Navy. The house has long been known as Quarters F, and now serves as home of the commander of the Naval Supply Center.

The First Dry Dock

To repair larger vessels, a shipyard must have a dry dock. Building the dry dock, in one of the biggest construction projects that had ever been undertaken in Charleston, became a first order of business for the new yard.[1]

Work was begun in November of 1902 by the contractor, the New York Continental Jewell Filtration Company. By 1905, the evacuation work had been completed and the first stones set in place. The dock was built of granite from the quarry at Winnsboro — 10,000 dressed stones

weighing an average of nearly two tons each. In March of 1907, the last of the huge blocks was cemented in place.

The specifications were impressive. The graving dock was 583 feet long and ninety-seven feet wide at the floor. It was the only dry dock in the United States made entirely of stone. Use of the dry dock would be delayed more than two years, however, until the yard powerhouse could be finished to supply electricity to the huge pumps.

The first dry-docking took place on 7 April 1909. It was a gala event with everyone at the yard from Rear Admiral Adams to the lowest-paid laborer in attendance. The dock was flooded and the

[1] A detailed photographic story of the construction of the dry dock is on exhibit at the Charleston Naval Shipyard Museum aboard the carrier *Yorktown* at Patriots Point Naval and Maritime Museum in Mount Pleasant, S. C.

caisson, the huge gate used to keep out the waters of the Cooper River, moved aside. At nine o'clock in the morning at high tide, five vessels entered the dock. They were the naval tug *Potomac*, the ferry tug *Kite*, two coal barges and the admiral's barge — the little steam launch *Courier*. The caisson was lowered into place and the three big pumps labored until midnight to drain the 25,000,000 gallons of water from the dock so work could begin.

The yard had waited a long time for the dry dock and in the first months it was used for a variety of vessels. The initial group stayed in dock only a few days and was followed by six torpedo boats, all docked at one time. Then came the hospital ship *Solace* followed by the battleship *Texas* and the protected cruiser *Atlanta*. With the new dry dock in operation, the Charleston Navy Yard was on its way to becoming a first-class ship repair facility for the Navy.

FIRST VESSELS TO ENTER DOCK AT NAVY YARD, CHARLESTON

"We called the big, steam-powered crane 'Monday.' It was so slow that whenever you wanted it on the other side of the dry dock, it would always be next Monday before it got there."

A. F. (Pee Wee) Ackerman

The first dry-docking at the Navy Yard took place on 7 April 1909. The large vessel is the naval tug Potomac. The others were a ferry tug, two coal barges, and the admiral's barge — the little steam launch Courier. Everyone at the yard from Rear Admiral Adams to the lowest-paid laborer was there when the vessels entered the dock at high tide at nine o'clock that morning. The big steam-powered crane on the left served at the yard more than forty years.

By October of 1905, construction of Dry Dock 1 was well underway. It was built of granite from the quarry at Winnsboro — 10,000 dressed stones weighing nearly two tons each. The last stone was set in place in April of 1907.

One of the first two civilian employees of the Navy Yard was Maxwell S. Crayton who was transferred from Port Royal to Charleston on 12 July 1902. Crayton was born in Pendleton, S. C. in 1878 and started work at Port Royal shortly after receiving his B.S. degree in civil and electrical engineering from South Carolina College. He served as chief draftsman at the yard for twenty-two years. This photograph was probably taken in 1936 when Crayton was the senior civilian assistant to the Public Works Officer.

The Texas lies at anchor in Hampton Roads in 1907 when she was part of the Coast Squadron. Not long afterwards, she became station ship at the yard where she served until early 1911. The 6,300-ton second-class battleship met her fate several years later when she was sunk as a target in Chesapeake Bay.

By 1909, five shop buildings had been completed including the Forge Shop, Building 6. Today the original shop buildings can be identified by their red brick construction.

Another of the original five shop buildings is the Shipfitters Shop, Building 2, shown in this postcard view. Added to several times since, the Shipfitters Shop remains one of the biggest facilities of its kind in the Southeast.

Cast ashore at the Navy Yard by the great hurricane of 1911 were these three torpedo boats. On 28 August the storm struck Charleston with 106-miles-per-hour winds, causing $1,000,000 worth of damage and ruining many rice fields in the Lowcountry. At the yard, the dry dock was flooded, a hundred trees uprooted, and the copper roof of Joiners Shop blown off. The submarine Tarantula and a torpedo boat were sunk at their moorings and the station ship Baltimore cast adrift.

A long line of battleships, eleven in fact, steams into Charleston Harbor on Sunday, 17 November 1912. They ranged in size from the Utah, the flagship of Rear Admiral Hugo Osterhaus at 21,825 tons, to the Illinois, at just over half that displacement. The big ships and the eleven thousand men who made up their crews stayed in Charleston for a week. They were lavishly entertained by the city, with events ranging from formal teas to football games. On Wednesday night, the officers attended a "splendid ball" given by the commandant and other officers of the Navy Yard. The visit of the battleships silenced critics of the harbor; for the North Dakota, the deepest-draft vessel, entered the harbor without difficulty while drawing 29.4 feet of water.

The old cruiser Baltimore was the station ship at the yard from early 1911 until September of 1912. When this photograph was made in 1913, she was laid up just prior to her conversion to a minelayer, which the yard completed the next year.

In 1913, the yard constructed its first vessels, two snag boats for the Corps of Engineers — the Pee Dee and the Wateree. Shown here is the Wateree, working in 1938 on the Congaree River. Such vessels were used to remove debris and obstructions from inland waters.

In 1912, the Navy's school for machinist mates was transferred from the Norfolk Navy Yard to Charleston. By July of 1913, when this photograph was taken in Building 9, there were 130 men enrolled.

These sailors were among those taught to be sea-going machinists in the yard's school. The training was thorough — the course took an entire year to complete.

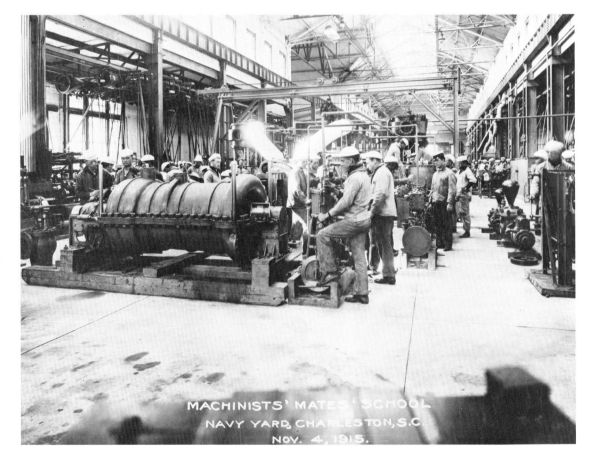

MACHINISTS' MATES' SCHOOL
NAVY YARD, CHARLESTON, S.C.
NOV. 4, 1915.

Several buildings were constructed to support the Machinist Mates School, including Building 11 shown here and later Building 10. By 1920, the machinist mates were gone and Building 11 had been turned into the Sheet Metal Shop and Building 10 was being used as the Pattern Shop and the Electric Shop.

In 1914, the Navy set up a clothing factory in Building 13, transferring this work from the Brooklyn Navy Yard. This project was a big success and several years later operations were expanded and an annex added to the clothing factory. During the First World War, a thousand women labored at their sewing machines at the yard, turning out dungarees, jumpers and other clothing for the Navy. Their salaries ranged from $1.04 to $3.52 per day.

A Magnificent Receiving Ship

She was famous as the flagship of Admiral David Farragut when he "damned the torpedos" and won the Battle of Mobile Bay. Her career spanned nearly a century, from the eve of the Civil War to the early years of the nuclear navy. But during her long naval service, the big, steam-powered sloop-of-war spent more time at the Charleston Navy Yard than anywhere else.

She was the *Hartford*, which arrived in Charleston in October of 1912. She became a fixture on the waterfront at the Navy Yard, as station ship and receiving ship for the Sixth Naval District. She remained at the yard until 1938 when, after being extensively refurbished, she finally left.

She was a big vessel for a wooden man-of-war, 225 feet long with a forty-four-foot beam and a displacement of 2,900 tons. Built in the Boston Navy Yard in 1858, she served in the Far East until the Civil War began. In January of 1862, she became Farragut's flagship of the West Gulf Blockading Squadron. Her wartime exploits made her one of the most famous American vessels of the period.

When the war ended, she returned to the Far East and later served as flagship of the North Atlantic Station. The last thirteen years before the turn of the century she spent at Mare Island, Admiral Farragut's old navy yard, where she was used as a training ship and later completely re-

built. In October of 1899, she returned to the Atlantic coast where she was used to train midshipmen until being transferred to Charleston in 1912, replacing the *Baltimore* as station ship.

At Charleston, she served as a home for officers and crewmen of ships at the yard and as headquarters for the Commandant of the Sixth Naval District. For those accustomed to the austerity of modern warships, *Hartford* would have seemed like heaven. In 1918, the young artist Norman Rockwell stayed aboard for a few weeks during his brief tour of duty at the Navy Yard. His description of the vessel:

> In the center of the ship a grand, red-carpeted staircase swept down to a huge ballroom whose walls were decorated with ornate, hand-carved scrollwork. The staterooms, which were the officers' quarters, were lavishly appointed and hung with all manner of rich velvets and tapestries. Down all the carpeted hallways ran handrails of gleaming brass. The kitchen . . . was staffed by a

horde of cooks — meat cooks, pastry cooks vegetable cooks, salad cooks, sauce cooks, etc. A marine band — scarlet jackets, blue trousers, white belts, and all — was kept always at readiness and marines in full-dress uniforms — dark blue coats, light blue trousers — guarded the gangplanks.

A far cry from the ship whose decks, a half-century earlier, had been piled with bodies and awash with blood as the forts of Mobile Bay and the vessels of the Confederate Fleet struck her mercilessly with a rain of shot and bursting shells!

The *Hartford* stayed at the yard through the twenties and the Depression years. In 1937 and 1938, she was extensively refurbished with funds provided by the WPA. The old vessel spent the next seven years in Washington, D. C. In 1945, she was moved to the Norfolk Naval Shipyard where she sank at her berth in 1956 and was subsequently dismantled.

On Washington's birthday in 1914, a plethora of flags ripple in the wind on two famous warships, then serving lighter duty. The big vessel in the center is the screw sloop-of-war Hartford, *the yard's receiving ship. Behind her is Admiral Dewey's famous flagship* Olympia, *her stacks showing above the Hartford's decks.*

In 1912, the old Hartford *became receiving ship at the yard, nearly a half-century after her exploits with Admiral David Farragut in the Battle of Mobile Bay. She became a fixture on the waterfront, staying at the yard until 1938.*

In December of 1914, the floating derrick Creighton was launched in the Cooper River. This vessel was built for the Corps of Engineers. The wooden structure behind the vessel is Building 1023, the yard recreational building. Behind it to the right is the Joiners Shop; the big building on the far right is the Machine Shop.

Admiral Dewey's flagship, the cruiser Olympia, lies quietly at a yard pier, circa 1915. She arrived at the yard in March of 1912 to serve as barracks ship for the Reserve Torpedo Group, a flotilla consisting of two destroyers, four submarines, and eight torpedo boats. The big cruiser was built in San Francisco in 1892. In 1898, at day break on the first day of May, Dewey gave his famous order, "You may fire when you are ready, Gridley" and the guns of Olympia and the other American vessels destroyed the Spanish Asian Fleet in the Battle of Manila Bay. The cruiser (the Navy's oldest steel warship) is still afloat, preserved as a shrine at Philadelphia.

The ferryboat Wave becomes the fourth vessel launched by the yard as she splashes into the Cooper River.

On 15 July 1915, the stern post for the tug Wando hangs from the crane as workmen get ready to move it to the building ways.

U.S. TUG "WANDO"
READY FOR LAUNCHING
MARCH 6, 1916.

On 6 March 1916, Wando is poised on the ways ready to be launched.

"Wando". Tug #17
Launched, Navy Yard, Charleston, S.C.
March 7, 1916.

The next day, with a number of spectators standing beside the recreational building watching, the tug slides into the Cooper River.

The yard engineering staff, office force, and inspectors, circa 1908.

One of the first buildings constructed at the Navy Yard was Quarters A, completed in 1905 as the home of the Navy Yard commandant. In 1945, it became the residence of the commander of the new Naval Base. The broad porches of the big house overlook fine gardens and the Cooper River.

Dry Dock Nº1, Oct. 2, 1915
showing
U.S.S. Olympia in Dock.

In October of 1915, the cruiser Olympia was in dry dock at the yard.

3

The Great War

During the First World War, many changes took place at the yard. The workforce nearly tripled in size. A naval training camp was established and a thousand-bed hospital built, which was needed due to the flu epidemics sweeping the country at the time. The yard built its first warships and repaired or converted many other vessels. Yard facilities were greatly expanded.

When war was declared by President Wilson in April of 1917, five German freighters interned in Charleston Harbor were seized by the government. Each of these vessels was overhauled by the yard and converted for naval use. Four were turned into transports. The other, the *Keil*, was converted into a submarine tender and renamed the *Camden* (AS-6). Many other naval vessels were repaired and overhauled by the yard during the war. These ranged from small craft and destroyers to the big cruiser *Denver*.

The yard also built ships. Eight wooden-hull submarine chasers were constructed, each 110 feet long with a displacement of eighty-five tons. The gunboat *Asheville* was built, although she was completed too late to see action in the war. Construction was also started on the *Tillman*, a destroyer named for the yard's benefactor in the United States Senate, who had died in July of 1918.

Also, during the war the yard's facilities were greatly improved. Buildings 10 and 11 were completed, the first yard structures made of reinforced concrete. Both were built for use of the Machinist Mates School. New building ways were also constructed along with a marine railway. A torpedo warehouse, Building 101, was built south of the yard. A new concrete pier (now Pier F) replaced a wooden one at the same site.

But the most ambitious construction project which was planned was never completed. This was a 1,000-foot dry dock, which was to be forty-four feet deep over the sill. Congress had authorized construction of the dry dock, along with a project to dredge the channel from the harbor entrance to the yard to a depth of forty feet. Before work could begin the war ended and these projects, along with others related to expansion of Navy facilities, were canceled by the Congress.

Yard employment during the war reached a peak of 5,600 people, 1,000 of whom worked in the Naval Clothing Factory. Another 5,000 men were at the Naval Training Camp adjacent to the yard.

In January of 1918, the light cruiser Albany *was in dry dock undergoing repairs.*

COMPLETE ASSOCIATED PRESS SERVICE

The News and Courier.

THE WEATHER
Washington, April 6.—Weather forecast for South Carolina. Fair and warmer Saturday; Sunday probably fair.

ESTABLISHED IN 1803.

CHARLESTON, S. C., SATURDAY MORNING, APRIL 7, 1917.

PRICE FIVE CENTS.

PRESIDENT WILSON SIGNS WAR DECLARATION; GOVERNMENT SEIZES INTERNED GERMAN SHIPS

WAR BILL SIGNED AMERICAN NATION TAKES UP SWORD

Word Flashed to All Army and Navy Stations and to Vessels at Sea

ORDERS FOR MOBILIZATION

Indications Are Brazil and Cuba Will Soon Follow United States in Declaring War on Germany

ARREST OF GERMAN PLOTTERS ORDERED

Sixty German Citizens Designated by Government as Engaged in Intrigue

BAIL WILL BE REFUSED

Indications are Other Arrests Will be Ordered Soon by Attorney General

Washington, April 6.—The arrest of sixty alleged ringleaders in German plots, conspiracies and machinations in the United States was ordered today by Attorney General Gregory immediately after President Wilson had signed the war resolution.

Every man whose arrest was ordered is a German citizen, is known by the Department of Justice. It was authoritatively stated, to have participated actively in German intrigue in this country and is regarded as a dangerous person to be at large.

Bail will be refused in each case. It was said, and the entire group will

TALKING REFORM IN GERMAN EMPIRE

America's Entry Into War Has Added Impetus to the Reform Movement

NO HOPE FOR VICTORY NOW

Growing Demand That Germany Follow Austria's Stand for Peace Minus Annexation

Copenhagen, April 6 (Via London). America's entry into the war evidently has had an immediate and strong effect on the reform movement, notes many.

The conviction that the instant modernisation of the Prussian Constitution and the proclamation of a more democratic basis of government and diplomacy in the Empire without waiting for the end of the war is necessary as a military and political measure to counteract the "tempest of the world's public opinion," as the Vorwaerts puts it, is evidently gaining

FRESH GAINS MADE BY ALLIED ARMIES

British Capture Lempiere, North of St. Quentin, inflicting Heavy Losses

FRENCH RECOVER GROUND

Russian and British Forces Unite in Mesopotamia, Turks in Retreat

British efforts to reach the Cambrai-St. Quentin high road and to drive a salient into the German lines between these two important points continue both continue successfully. In operations near Ronssoy, ten miles north of St. Quentin, Field Marshal Haig's men have captured Lempiere, five miles east of the Cambrai-St. Quentin road and thirteen miles southwest of Cambrai. Prisoners were taken by the British and large numbers of German dead are reported by London to have been found in the captured positions.

The Germans lost severely in the operations between Arras and St. Quentin during the last week.

TO USE INTERNED SHIPS TO CARRY ARMS TO ALLIES

Hundred German Merchantmen Taken Over By United States in Various Ports

MOST OF VESSELS DAMAGED

Ships Seized Will Likely Be Regarded as Government Property to Be Paid for After the War

Courtesy the Charleston News and Courier

America enters the great war. There were five interned German vessels in Charleston Harbor that were seized.

The German freighter Nicaria was converted by the yard to a naval transport and renamed the Pensacola (AK-7).

The yard converted the Keil, another seized German vessel, into one of the early submarine tenders.

Here the Keil, renamed the Camden (AS-6) lies at a yard pier in August of 1917.

In 1917, Building 7 (on the left) contained the offices of the Supply Department. The yard industrial offices were in Building 8 across the street. Both buildings were also used for storage.

The German freighter Liebenfels was converted by the yard to serve as a naval transport and renamed Houston (AK-1). The Liebenfels was scuttled in Charleston Harbor by her crew in an attempt to block the channel and had to be raised before she could be taken to the yard.

The big cruiser Denver was in dry dock in February of 1918. She spent the war escorting convoys of merchant ships from New York and Norfolk to mid-Atlantic where destroyers took over the task on the remainder of the voyage to Europe.

The yard waterfront in November of 1918. The marine railway is in the center of the picture. The vessel in the right background is the gunboat Asheville.

Building The Yard's First Warship

The keel for the gunboat Asheville was laid at the yard on 9 June 1917. She was the first major United States warship to be built in Charleston in more than a century.

On the fourth of July 1918, Asheville is ready for launching. She was christened, not with traditional champagne, but with a bottle of pure water from a mountain stream at the North Carolina city for which she was named.

Members of the Asheville launching crew stand by awaiting the signal for the big gunboat to begin sliding down the ways.

Her flags rippling in a stiff breeze, Asheville slides into the Cooper River. Hers was one of many launchings at shipyards throughout the country on Independence Day in 1918.

In November of 1918, Asheville was in dry dock for final fitting-out. She was 241 feet long with a forty-one-foot beam, displacing 1,207 tons. Her armament consisted of three four-inch guns.

The gunboat spent most of her time in the 1930s in Chinese waters. She was sunk by a Japanese squadron south of Java on 3 March 1942.

The Naval Training Camp

In 1917, a naval training camp was established at the yard. Named Camp Bagley, it was located west of the hospital reservation on property leased from the city of Charleston.

The camp stood between St. John's Avenue, then named Cosgrove, and Spruill Avenue. In early 1919 it was moved across the railroad tracks into Piney Grove, the present site of Ben Tillman Homes. This area was part of the original Chicora Park tract owned by the city.

During the First World War, the camp was a busy place with up to 5,000 recruits from around the country in residence at a time. It provided basic training for young men who were to serve the Navy in various capacities, such as naval aviators, "flying stevedores" and machinist mates who would enter the school at the yard.

The facilities were hardly sumptuous. Knocked-together wooden barracks provided space for about a thousand men. The rest slept in tents pitched among the tall pine trees.

Life at the camp for a new recruit began with a twenty-one day "detention period," during which time he couldn't leave the camp. According to artist Norman Rockwell, a new man might be assigned sentry duty, standing in the mud in a drizzle watching for Germans. He might pull stumps to clear an area to build new barracks. Some were assigned burial detail digging graves in the old cemetery on the north side of Turnbull Avenue for boys who died of the flu. And everyone learned the rudiments of being a sailor — how

BIRD'S EYE VIEW OF TRAINING CAMP

Courtesy South Carolina Historical Society.

In 1918, there were 5,000 men at the Naval Training Camp at the yard. The upper view is looking north. The railroad tracks now run parallel to Spruill Avenue in North Charleston. The bottom view is looking southeast. The athletic fields used by the sailors are on the upper right.

to salute, how to march, and how to play baseball.

Indeed, sports were a big part of camp life, particularly baseball, football and boxing. Baseball teams from the training camp and the receiving ship *Hartford* took on teams from The Citadel, Fort Moultrie and Parris Island. Boxing matches drew big crowds. The playing fields were located south of Third Street, an area now occupied by warehouses and the yard outer parking lot. Also here were the YMCA, the YWCA and the Knights of Columbus hut. Entertainment nearby for the recruits was important, for much of the time they were quarantined to the base because of flu epidemics.

The welfare of the recruits was a big concern to Charlestonians. Free dances were put on at places such as Hibernian Hall. Enlisted men's clubs abounded. The YMCA sponsored a Navy newspaper *Afloat and Ashore*, which was printed by the Charleston *News and Courier*. Nor were the women, most serving as yeomenettes, neglected.

Mr. and Mrs. John D. Rockefeller, Jr. came to town to dedicate the new Eliza Lucas Hall YWCA building at the yard, one of the finest such facilities in America.

The first commandant of the camp was Lieutenant Commander Morrison. He was succeeded by Commander (later Captain) Mark St. Clair Ellis. Among other things, Ellis had purchased the camp's most unusual residents — a hundred hogs kept penned under the tall pine trees in Piney Grove to supply fresh pork for the men. His wife, a well-to-do woman said to be the first in America to earn a mining degree, was particularly popular with the men. She often passed out awards for athletic contest winners and bought equipment such as movie projectors needed at the camp.

Shortly after the war ended, the camp was disbanded and when the Navy's lease expired, the property where the camp stood returned to the City of Charleston.

Courtesy South Carolina Historical Society.

A sentry stands guard beside the road through the Naval Training Camp. This road is now St. John's Avenue; then it was called Cosgrove Ave.

The Naval Training Camp was moved in early 1919 across the railroad tracks to the site where Ben Tillman Homes now stand. As many as 4,000 men lived in tents here during the First World War.

The conclusion of a boxing match between recruits at the Naval Training Camp. Sports — particularly baseball, football, and boxing — were considered an important part of camp life in developing the young men.

THE COMMANDER'S POLICY

It must be evident that I have been detailed to command the Training Camp here in order to perfect the organization best suited to the development of its usefulness and the instruction of its highly intelligent but untrained young men.

To reach such a large body of men, nearly 5,000, it is manifest that I must use an organized force of trained officers and chief petty officers, since no one man could reach each individual in this command.

If these officers and chief petty officers are acquainted with my ideals and aims for this camp it will help them to direct every energy toward achieving the high standard set. Therefore, a few words as to my policy seem appropriate.

Each officer and each petty officer must exert himself to instill and keep up a camp spirit of cheerful willingness.

If there be any one in authority "pulling back" he must be relegated to other fields; if there be a man in training who is cross-grained and is "knocking" those in authority over him he must be eliminated from the finest navy on earth and be sent to the draft boards.

Volunteers should be cheerful.

All should remember that a hundred men desire the place of every aviator in training.

Modern methods of training suited to the modern man will be employed here.

If you deserve it, "young aviator in the making," you will be treated like an under classman at the Naval Academy rather than like the old-time naval apprentice boy.

In the short time we keep you here we want you first to learn how to keep your body and your clothes clean and neat under the difficult conditions of hard service. We want you to learn how to defend yourself with the rifle, the bayonet, and the pistol. We want you to learn how to row a boat and how to swim and play baseball and football.

We want you to learn, above all else, correct military deportment; how to salute and how to honor your country's flag; how to salute your officers—looking them squarely in the eye while so doing—as much as to say, "Mr. Officer, I am just as proud of my blue jacket's clothes as you are of your uniform, because it means that I, too, have volunteered to serve the country in this great war."

Somebody has to do the work in the lower ratings, so why not you. Try to make it said of the bluejacket in this day what was current in the palmy days of ancient Rome, "When to be a Roman soldier was greater than to be a King."

Of all men on earth I love the American bluejackets most. Therefore, it is but fitting that I should command so many of you. My doors swing wide open to each and all of you for any purpose of duty, efficiency, happiness and betterment.

It will aoffrd us all pleasure and profit to read and support *Afloat and Ashore* and to mail it to the folks at home.

In conclusion, let me state that I esteem it a great honor to serve again under our commandant, Rear Admiral F. E. Beatty, U. S. N. He was my instructor at the Naval Academy when I was your age.

Commander Mark St. Clare Ellis, U. S. N.,
Commandant Naval Training Camp.

Commander Ellis' guidance to the men when he took over in 1918.

Men of the Naval Training Camp sit down to Thanksgiving dinner in 1918. In the right foreground of the upper photograph is Commander Mark St. Clair Ellis, Commandant of the Training Camp and the receiving ship Hartford.

Mrs. Ellis passes out prize money to winners of sports competitions at the Training Camp. According to Norman Rockwell, she was loved by the men and often bought things such as movie projectors for the camp with her own money.

A Navy Yard Artist

On 23 August 1918, a skinny, serious-minded young man from New Rochelle, New York reported to the Naval Training Camp at the yard. New recruits arrived from around the country almost every day, so this event was hardly out of the ordinary. The recruit, however, was. At the age of twenty-three, he was already a famous artist. His name was Norman Rockwell.

Had it not been for a bunch of bananas and a German submarine, Rockwell would have never made it to Charleston.

When he went to enlist in the Navy, he was found to be underweight. Not one to be easily deterred from something he had set his mind to, Rockwell agreed to undergo "the treatment" at the recruiting office. This consisted of stuffing himself with bananas and doughnuts and drinking all the water he could hold in order to gain seven pounds. The treatment worked and Rockwell, so full he could scarcely walk, signed up.

He was ordered to report to the Brooklyn Navy Yard. From there he was to ship out to a base in Ireland where he was to paint insignia on airplanes. His ship sailed at night, with Rockwell standing on deck watching the lights of New York City. But before the vessel left the harbor, it was stopped by an American submarine. The submarine commander ordered the ship's captain to sail south to Charleston to avoid a German submarine which was lying off the coast.

Shortly after his arrival in Charleston, young Rockwell found out that he was not about to be treated as an ordinary recruit. As he later told it:

> In the morning we filled out questionnaires on our civilian work experience and training. I put down 'illustrator.' The chief petty officer, who was looking over the questionnaires, asked if I would do his portrait. I did. That afternoon an ensign saw the portrait and asked if I'd draw him. I did. He showed it to a captain and the captain called me into his office. I entered in my new uniform — bell-bottom trousers, tight blouse, and little white cap; I looked like a toadstool turned upside down. The captain said, 'Oh, my God,' and assigned me to the camp newspaper, *Afloat and Ashore*, giving me ten days' leave to go to New York and get my art supplies. 'Your job's morale,' he said. 'You'll do more good that way than swabbing decks or stoking boilers.' As I left the room he added, 'You'd make a helluva sailor anyway.'

Rockwell's job consisted of drawing cartoons and making layouts for *Afloat and Ashore*, which took him two days each week. The rest of the time he was allowed to work on whatever he wanted so long as it related to the Navy. He therefore was able to continue his work on covers for *Post* and *Life* by making sure that each one had a naval theme, which, of course, was easy to do in wartime. He also painted innumerable portraits of officers at the Yard.

One of these, he said, even saved his life. As he recalled in his autobiography:

> I have to admit that doing portraits of officers made my life less complicated. If I wanted a pass to town I'd just ask one of my sitters. He could hardly refuse; I might have elongated his nose or weakened his chin. One portrait I did even saved my life. When I caught the flu I went to the hospital. A doctor whose portrait I had drawn discovered me there. 'Get out of here,' he said. 'The place'll kill you. The germs are as thick as blackstrap molasses in here. Go back to your hammock and pile blankets on yourself. Sweat it out.' I did as he directed and recovered.

FAMOUS ARTIST IS IN TRAINING CAMP

Norman Rockwell Now In the Fourth Regiment

Norman Rockwell, who has been employed on the art editorial staff of the Saturday Evening Post for the post few years, is now in training in the Fourth regiment. His home is in New Rochelle, N. Y. He reported for duty at the Naval Training Station on August 23, 1918.

Rockwell attended the Art Students' League and also the National Academy of Design, where he made splendid records and very soon began to take a place among the artists of the day. His paintings have appeared on the covers of most all the popular magazines, such as the American Magazine, Popular Magazine, Red Cross Magazine, Leslie's, Judge, Life, the Country Gentlemen and The Saturday Evening Post. Besides painting for magazines, a large part of his time has been devoted to war work posters, and proven a valuable aid in recruiting for the army and navy and the Red Cross.

A few of his "big hits" are: "A Tribute From France," Judge, August 10, 1918; "Till the Boys Come Home," Life, August 15, 1918; cover of The Saturday Evening Post, May 18, 1918; cover of The Country Gentlemen, December 22, 1917.

Through his experience in designing and painting, he hopes to join the camouflage section, where he would prove a valuable man.

Afloat and Ashore, courtesy Library of Congress.

On 23 August 1918, young Norman Rockwell arrived at the Naval Training camp at the yard. At the age of twenty-three, he was already a well-known artist.

Catching the flu back then was serious business. Most of the period Rockwell was at the yard the sailors were quarantined to the base. In his words, "flu was raging through the camp like a pack of rabid wolves; men were dying every day."

Several months after Rockwell arrived in Charleston, Commander Mark St. Clair Ellis took over command of the Naval Training Camp. Rockwell's first meeting with Commander Ellis took place in the artist's studio, where he and his buddy, a sailor named O'Toole, were discussing the new commander. As Rockwell told it,

One afternoon O'Toole and I were in my studio discussing the situation when the door was suddenly flung open, a voice yelled 'A-ten-shun!' and in walked the new commander in full-dress uniform — white jacket and trousers, gold braid and white gloves — a big, handsome, beefy-looking fellow. His wife — a square, mannish lady smartly dressed — accompanied him.

'Carry on, men, carry on,' he said. I went back to work on the portrait I was painting and O'Toole fussed with a pile of old canvases in the corner. The new commander stood behind me, looking at the portrait.

After a minute I happened to glance around and saw that he was leaning on my palette table, one of his white-gloved hands squished down in the gobs and smears of oil paint. Oh, Lord, I thought, Siberia, here I come. 'Ah, Commander, sir,' I said, 'your hand, sir. Paint, sir.' He lifted his hand and looked at the glove, sticky with paint of many colors. I composed a brave farewell letter to my friends at home. But then he laughed and, stripping off his glove, said, 'A souvenir,' and handed it to me. He chatted a bit, asking about my work and how I liked the navy, and left the room. O'Toole was of the opinion that the new commander could be 'got round,' but, he added; 'the wife was a fish of a different color!'

The next day, Rockwell was transferred to Commander Ellis' personal staff and moved his studio aboard the *Hartford* where Ellis had his headquarters. His job was painting portraits of the commander and his wife.

Not long afterwards the war ended. On 12 November 1918, the day after the Armistice, Rockwell was discharged and his brief career in the Navy came to an end.

Rockwell's official duties consisted of drawing cartoons for the camp newspaper, Afloat and Ashore. The figure in the center is said to be a self-portrait; he declared that in his new uniform he looked like a "toadstool turned upside down."

Afloat and Ashore, courtesy Library of Congress.

Another Rockwell cartoon lampooned the twenty-one-day detention period which all new recruits underwent after arrival at the camp.

THE SATURDAY
EVENING POST

The Norman Rockwell Museum, Stockbridge, Mass.

While at the yard, Rockwell was allowed to continue his work for Post and Life so long as it had a naval theme. It was said that with his magazine commissions he made more money than an admiral.

The Norman Rockwell Museum.

Along with his other duties, Rockwell painted portraits of officers at the yard, for which he was not paid except in the good will of his superiors.

The Marshlands Plantation house (center background) was surrounded by diverse activities in September of 1918. To the right is Building 13, the Naval Clothing Factory. On the far right is Building 9, home of the Machinist Mates School, Pattern Shop, Boiler Shop and the Foundry. The big vessel on the left is the Asheville.

The crew of the Boiler Shop, circa 1918, looks as though it could take on any job. The man in the long-sleeved shirt in the center of the second row is Robert Flagg Ilderton, shop master.

In the summer of 1918, the main gate of the yard seems like a leisurely place for a girl to chat with a sailor. The gate was located about where the Third Street gate now stands.

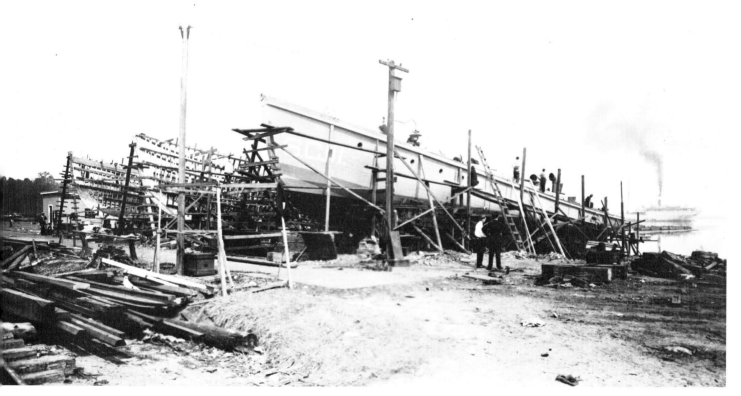

The yard built eight wooden-hull submarine chasers during the First World War. Each vessel was 110 feet long and powered by three gasoline engines. Some 121 American sub chasers, and one hundred more built for the French, hunted German U-boats in European waters before the Armistice.

In 1919, the Georgia was at the yard for coaling. The battleship displaced 15,000 tons and carried a crew of 812 men. She spent much of 1919 ferrying troops home from Europe.

By 1917, the Naval Clothing Factory had outgrown Building 13 and a large annex to the building was in use as well.

The Seven Subs in Dry Dock.
Navy Yard. Charleston. S.C.
After Flooding
Photo by Hildebrandt.
Passed by The Chief Naval Censor

The yard repaired submarines as early as 1911. Here in 1919 there are seven in drydock at one time.

In March of 1936, workmen pave a road near Building 30. During the
Depression, millions of federal relief dollars poured into Charleston
in the form of WPA and PWA projects at the Navy Yard.

4

Between Wars

After the signing of the Armistice, activity at the yard began to wind down. The Great War was over. The nation entered a period of peace and prosperity in the 1920s and turned its attention to the Good Life. While people danced the Charleston, the Charleston Navy Yard withered and almost died.

But during the Great Depression, changes came at the yard. Ships were built and millions of dollars poured into improved facilities, creating thousands of jobs for out-of-work Charlestonians. By the time the German blitzkrieg was unleashed in Poland in the autumn of 1939, Charleston had a first-class navy yard.

After the First World War ended, the satellite functions at the yard were the first to go. The Naval Clothing Factory was shut down. The Machinist Mates School returned to the Norfolk Navy Yard and the Naval Training Camp was closed.

For several years the yard continued to build vessels. In 1919, two tugs, two coal barges and an ammunition lighter were launched. The gunboat *Asheville* was completed and construction was begun on a similar vessel, the *Tulsa*. The yard's first destroyer, the *Tillman*, was launched in July of 1919.

The *Tillman*, typical of the four-stack destroyers of World War I, was 314.4 feet long with a displacement of 1,090 tons. Carrying a crew of 122 officers and men, she could make thirty-four knots. Much of her career was spent in training cruises for naval reservists and NROTC midshipmen. In late 1940, she was one of fifty old destroyers turned over to the British in exchange for American leases on sites for bases on British soil. She was commissioned HMS *Wells* in the Royal Navy and saw considerable action in World War II.

As the ship construction program wound down in the years following the First World War, workload at the yard dropped. In 1922, the Navy decided to close the Charleston yard.

The order was signed by Franklin D. Roosevelt as acting Secretary of the Navy on 10 July 1922. It provided for shutting down the yard as soon as practicable, after finishing the *Tulsa* to a point where she could be towed to another navy yard. The tentative closing date was set as 1 September, less than three months away.

Reaction from Charlestonians was predictable. The Chamber of Commerce made an appeal to keep the yard open. Charleston leaders, aided by Senator "Cotton Ed" Smith, carried the fight to Washington and persuaded the Navy Department and President Harding not to close the yard. Their strongest argument was the strategic location of the yard, as the southernmost on the Atlantic Seaboard and the only one between the Virginia Capes and the Gulf of Mexico. By 1924, however, employment at the yard had dropped to only 479 people. During this period, Tom McMillan, U. S. Congressman from the Charleston district, emerged as the Navy Yard's chief defender.

For the next few years, the yard maintained a core of experienced people in each trade. The workload mainly consisted of routine upkeep on minesweepers and tugboats. By 1932, yard employment was still holding steady at about 515 civilian workers and twenty-six naval officers.

Good news came in 1933 when the Navy designated Charleston a new construction yard. Soon the welcome sounds of riveting and hammering steel plate returned to the waterfront along with the bright glow of the welder's torch. The first vessels built were three small Coast Guard cutters, launched in September of 1934, an event, according to the commandant, which marked "the rebirth of the Charleston Navy Yard as a producing plant."

Additional construction work quickly followed. Another, much bigger, Coast Guard cutter named the *Bibb* was built along with the gunboat *Charleston*. Several yard tugboats were also built. The first of a series of destroyers, the *Sterett*, was constructed followed by the *Roe* (DD-418).[1] On the eve of the Second World War, the *Hillary P. Jones* and the *Grayson* were on the building ways and the yard had contracts for two additional destroyers.

As the shipbuilding got underway, work began on improvements to the yard's facilities. A massive program of public works projects was undertaken as part of the nationwide relief effort. In the late 1930s as many as 1,800 previously out-of-work Charlestonians were working on

---

[1] A photo essay on construction of the *Roe* is on display at the shipyard Museum aboard the carrier *Yorktown*.

The Tillman , the first destroyer built by the yard, surges through New York Harbor. In 1940, she was one of fifty old U. S. destroyers given to England in exchange for rights to establish American bases on British soil. She served in World War II as HMS Wells.

yard facilities for fifty-seven dollars a month. These projects were sponsored by the Work Projects Administration and the Public Works Administration, which were created by Roosevelt to help the nation get back on its feet.

The improved facilities helped get the yard on its feet as a first-class construction and repair shipyard. New shipbuilding ways were built. The Structural Shop and the Machine Shop were expanded and other shop buildings improved. Streets were paved and new railroad tracks laid. New cranes were built and better machine tools installed.

By 1939, civilian employment at the yard had increased to 2,395 people, the most since late 1919. Training of workers had improved also with the new apprentice program started in 1935.

Efforts at improvements in the late 1930s were aided by an organization of yard employees called the Navy Yard Development Association. This group was established on 14 January 1937 and by the end of the year more than 800 workers were members. Among its concerns were means to improve the yard and increase its employment and workload. The association sponsored a visit by a huge congressional party in 1938 that is described elsewhere in this chapter. Each year a handsome booklet was published describing the yard and the major events of the past year. The association remained active until the end of the Second World War.

The Turnbull Avenue gate looking northeast in February of 1921.

The Cole, a four-stack destroyer which was a frequent visitor to the
yard, lies serenely at a yard pier.

Courtesy the Charleston News and Courier.

The yard fire department stands ready for any conflagration in this 1930s view. The man on the motorcycle is Norman A. Miller who served as chief of police and fire chief at the Navy Yard for thirty-five years.

The Dispensary, Building 19, once stood where Building 234, the yard headquarters, is now located. In 1922 when this photograph was taken, the Dispensary had sixty-eight beds. Not long afterwards the 1,000-bed World War I emergency hospital was torn down and the Dispensary became the yard hospital.

The Navy Yard, circa 1930. Look carefully and you can see a ship entering the dry dock. The Hartford is moored by the quay wall at the lower right of the picture.

The Coast Guard harbor cutter Navesink was one of three such vessels under construction in Dry Dock 1 in July of 1934. According to the commandant, the launching of the three cutters two months later marked "the rebirth of the Charleston Navy Yard as a producing plant."

Miss Katherine Reynolds christens the Coast Guard cutter George M. Bibb as it starts down the ways on 14 January 1937.

Between 1933 and 1937, the yard built four Coast Guard cutters, the largest of which was the 2000-ton Bibb.

In February of 1936, work proceeds on the gunboat Charleston, the
biggest vessel yet constructed by the yard. She was 328.5 feet long
with a displacement of 2,000 tons. The fourth naval vessel to bear the
name Charleston, she carried a crew of 236 officers and men and
was armed with four six-inch guns.

On 10 October 1936, the Charleston is
preparing to begin her shakedown
cruise. Much of her wartime service
was spent patrolling off the Alaskan
coast.

In May of 1936, workmen were paving the road that became Hobson Avenue.

Yard improvement projects included a greenhouse, shown here in November of 1937.

The public works projects included improvements to the waterfront. The old Hartford, in the center of the picture, is moored at her usual spot. Pier F is to the right. Not long after this 1938 photograph was taken, the Hartford was moved into dry dock for an extensive refurbishment.

Another PWA project was construction of new shipbuilding ways. By June of 1939 the new building ways had been essentially completed. The little pier in the upper part of the picture is located where the original wharf at Chicora Park once stood. It was here that President Theodore Roosevelt and Mayor Smyth boarded the Algonquin in 1902.

In June of 1939, work continues between Building 4 and Building 8.
The little structure in the left foreground was the police station. It
once stood on South Battery Street at White Point Gardens as the
ticket office for the Charleston horsedrawn railway.

Another PWA project was rehabilitation of the Hartford. In August of 1938 she was in dry dock for repairs to the hull.

In this view, the copper sheathing on the bottom of the vessel can be seen. The practice of using copper on ships hulls to reduce fouling and protect against shipworms was started before the American Revolution.

This is what the boiler room on the Hartford looked like as the vessel was being refurbished by the yard in the fall of 1938. It was said that the project was undertaken because President Franklin D. Roosevelt fell in love with the old ship during a visit to the Navy Yard.

These men were the first officers of the Navy Yard Development Association. Left to right are Treasurer Seth J. Ferrara, chief clerk of the Industrial Department; Vice-President Edward P. Harvey, who was a planner and estimator; President Simon Sorentru, master mechanic of the power plant; and the Secretary James L. Madden, quarterman joiner. The association was formed in January of 1937 to promote improvements at the yard.

The Navy Yard Development Association float in the Azalea Festival parade in 1938.

The Roe ready for launching. The destroyer initially was armed with five five-inch guns and twelve torpedo tubes. During the war, one five-inch gun and four torpedo tubes were removed in favor of anti-aircraft guns and additional electronic gear.

The Roe was launched on 21 June 1939. She was commissioned the next January and saw considerable action during World War II.

This cup was presented to the Roe's sponsor, Mrs. Eleanor Roe Hilton, by the shipyard employees at the vessel's launching ceremony.

Looking south across the yard in August of 1936. The Marshlands Plantation house can be seen among the oak trees in the background.

One standing atop the roof of Building 2 on 3 August 1936 was presented with this tranquil view of the yard waterfront.

The Great Congressional Visit

Over the years the yard has had many distinguished visitors. In 1984, for example, eleven senior naval officers, the Under Secretary of the Navy, and Senator Ernest Hollings were among those who visited the yard. But never in the yard's history has there been anything to match the great congressional visit of 1938, when, it seems, half the officials in Washington, D. C. must have come to Charleston.

The visit took place on 23 April, during Charleston's annual Azalea Festival. The guests arrived on the "Congressional Special," a chartered train from the nation's capitol.

Heading the group was Vice-President John Garner. Twelve U. S. senators came, most accompanied by their wives. The South Carolina senators Ellison D. "Cotton Ed" Smith and James F. Byrnes, of course, were present, along with a feisty former haberdasher from Missouri named Harry S Truman.

No fewer than seventy members of the House were in the party, nearly all with their wives. Tom McMillan from the Charleston district was there, as was Carl Vinson from Georgia, Chairman of the Naval Affairs Committee. From Texas came Sam Rayburn, Democratic floor leader of the House, who was serving his thirteenth term in Congress. Also from Texas was a first-term congressman named Lyndon B. Johnson, accompanied by his young wife with the strange name of Lady Bird.

Other guests ranged from Daniel Roper, the Secretary of Commerce, to the Deputy Commissioner of the Bureau of Fisheries, to Miss Washington of 1938. The press corps, of course, could not ignore such an event and they arrived in force with many newspapers, such as the *New York Times* and the *Christian Science Monitor*, represented.

The party reached the yard about 1:30 p.m. that Saturday afternoon. First on the agenda was a luncheon served at the yard cafeteria. There each guest was presented a copy of the Navy Yard Development Association Navy Day booklet of 1937. Tom McMillan, who had helped set up the visit, made a short speech.

After lunch, the party went to the building ways for the laying of the keel of the destroyer *Roe*. Vice-President Garner gave a short talk to the assembled yard workers and then drove the first

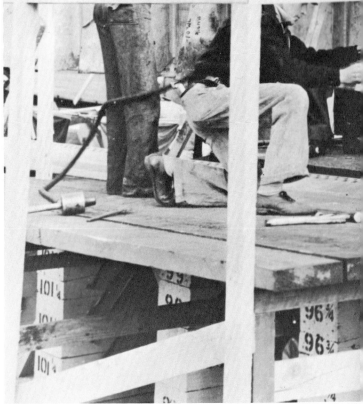

rivet in the keel with the help of Senator Smith, Senator Byrnes and Congressman Vinson. To provide souvenirs of the occasion, the rivet was split into four parts and each mounted on a wooden base made from a timber of the *Hartford*, which the yard was restoring at the time. These were presented to the four guests. The Vice-President called his "a reminder of a most pleasing experience."

The visit concluded with a tour of the yard with the guests in four Greyhound buses. Congressman McMillan later wrote to Rear Admiral Allen, the Navy Yard Commandant, saying that he was "certain the efforts put forth in making this trip possible will be returned to us in many ways in the years to come."

The keel laying ceremony for the Roe (DD-418) drew many distinguished guests on 23 April 1938. The bare-headed man on the left in the light-colored suit is Vice-President John Garner. To the right of the naval officer standing beside him are Senator James F. Byrnes, Senator Ellison D. Smith, Congressman Carl Vinson, Charleston Mayor Burnett Maybank, Rear Admiral Allen, and Congressman Thomas McMillan. The visitors were among the many guests who came to the yard during the Azalea Festival of 1938.

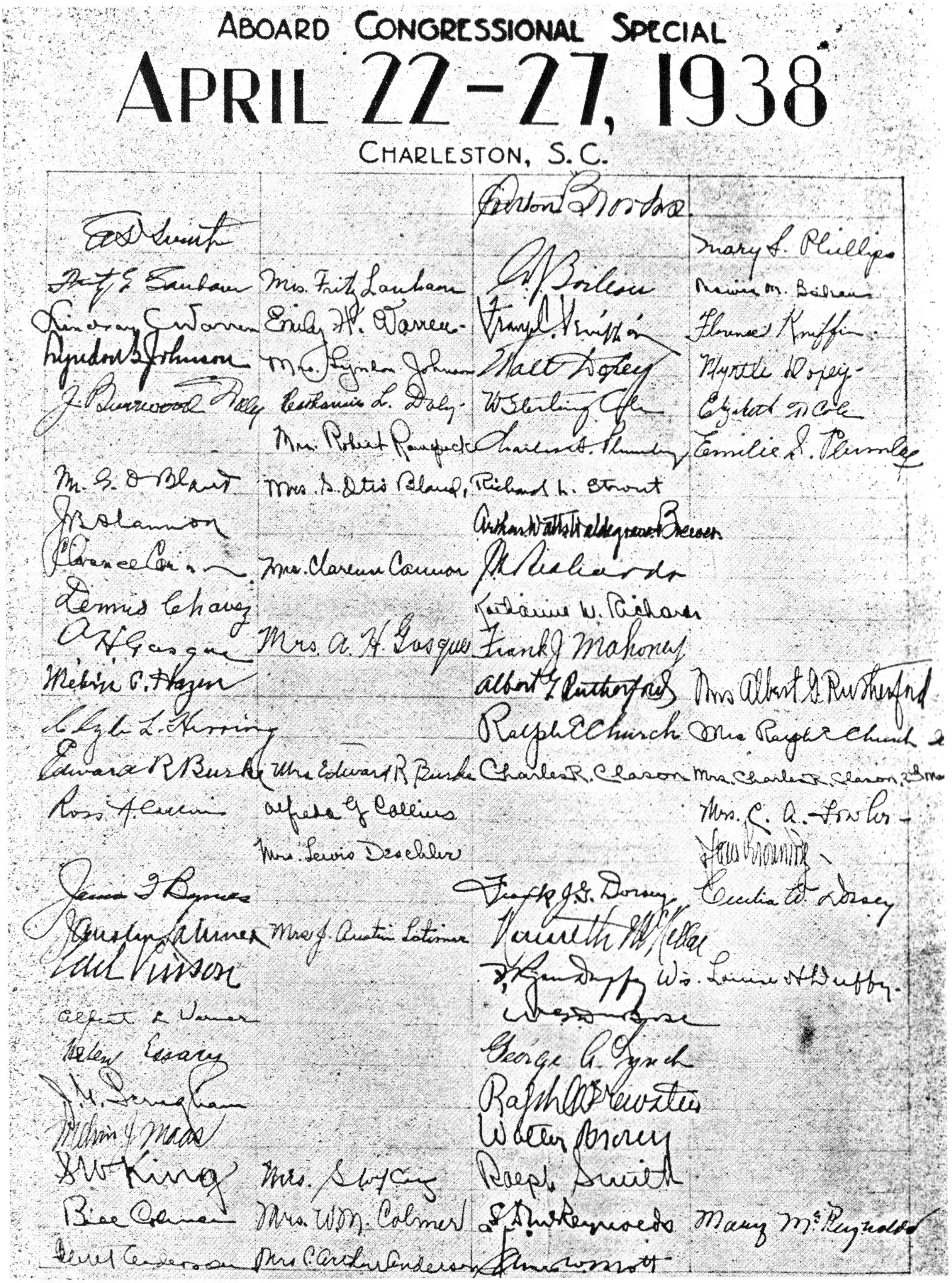
ABOARD CONGRESSIONAL SPECIAL
APRIL 22-27, 1938
CHARLESTON, S.C.

Autographs of members of the congressional party who visited the Navy Yard on 23 April 1938. Among the visitors were Senator Harry S Truman and two congressmen from Texas, Sam Rayburn, the House Democratic leader, and a young first-term congressman named Lyndon B. Johnson who was accompanied

FIFTH ANNUAL
AZALEA FESTIVAL
NAVY YARD DEVELOPMENT ASSOCIATION

by his wife Lady Bird. John B. Hartnett obtained the autographs for the Navy Yard Development Association by boarding the "Congressional Special" train at Florence early that morning.

Members of the Supply Department office staff in Building 7 in August of 1938.

Rear Admiral William Henry Allen, a native of Florence, S. C., was Commandant of the Yard on the eve of the Second World War. He served as commandant more than four years. Only Rear Admiral B. C. Bryan of the World War I period served longer as commandant or shipyard commander.

Tom McMillan, U. S. congressman from the Charleston district, was one of the leading supporters of the yard for many years. He helped keep the yard open in the mid-1920s.

In the late 1930s, President Franklin D. Roosevelt made two separate visits to the yard to check on the progress of the modernization program.

President Roosevelt and South Carolina governor Olin D. Johnston (center) converse in an open automobile during one of the President's visits to the yard. On Governor Johnston's right is Charleston Mayor Burnett Maybank.

5

The Second World War

During World War II, the Navy Yard became the largest employer, public or private, that the state has ever known. Ships were built in unprecedented numbers: in 1944 alone 116 new vessels splashed into the waters of the Cooper River. A complete new shipyard was constructed to support a crash program for building destroyer escorts. Besides building ships, the yard repaired and converted hundreds of vessels, not only American warships but also vessels of eight foreign countries.

THE PEOPLE

In 1939 when Hitler invaded Poland, the yard had approximately 2,400 workers, the result of a gradual buildup in the late 1930s. Nearly all were employed in the new construction program, building the destroyers *Sterett* and *Roe* and several tugs.

The next year, American involvement in the European war increased — primarily with aid to Great Britain. Industry of the "great arsenal of democracy" was put on a war footing. The Bureau of Ships told the navy yards to hire people as fast as possible.

This was easier said than done. The peacetime civil service regulations didn't lend themselves to hiring and processing the enormous numbers of workers needed. With limited ability to recruit and advertise, the yard found it difficult to compete with private industry. But the people came. Employment in 1941 was up to nearly 9,000. In July of 1943 it reached its peak when an incredible total of 25,943 people worked at the yard.

They came from all over: fishermen from the Lowcountry, farmers and mill hands from the Piedmont, people from Conway, Spartanburg, Ninety-Six, and Round O. They came from Georgia, Tennessee, North Carolina, Kentucky, Mississippi, and nearly every other state in the Union. At first there was a good deal of inefficiency as the thousands of untrained workers were assimilated into the work force. Things gradually improved, however, to the point where the yard won the coveted Army-Navy "E" award for efficiency five times straight.

At first, prospective new employees were required to meet the high physical standards of the peacetime civil service. Later a more realistic policy was adopted and handicapped people who could do the work were actively recruited. Many of these were returning war veterans who had left the yard previously to join the armed services.

In July of 1941, Miss Jean Corry does the honors as the Corry (DD-463) is ready to slide down the ways. On D-day, 6 June 1944, the destroyer struck a mine in the English Channel and sank. Many of her survivors were picked up by the Hobson (DD-464), her Charleston-built sister ship.

Rigger Herman E. Stanaland displays his war bonds. Bond drives were held frequently during the war years. Millions of dollars in war bonds were purchased by yard workers.

In all, 4,047 yard workers joined the military during the course of the war. Shops posted honor rolls of their men who had left to fight. In early 1944, often more than one hundred workers per week joined up.

Many of the men who left were replaced by women. During the war thousands of women worked at the Navy Yard. Their story is told elsewhere in this chapter.

Finding adequate housing for the workers was a big problem. The Navy did what it could to help locate available housing. Eventually thousands of new homes for the workers were built in the North Area. The George Legare, Ben Tillman, and Tom McMillan apartment projects were built near the yard on property owned by the city of Charleston as part of the old Chicora Park tract. Liberty Homes and Liberty Homes Extension were constructed. Much of what eventually became the city of North Charleston was built during the war to support the Navy Yard.

Not only was the work force dramatically expanded, but each worker was also required to work more hours. In January of 1942, the yard was placed on a three-shift-per-day, seven-day week. Each employee worked forty-eight hours during the week with staggered days off. This arrangement didn't work out efficiently and it was changed so that each person worked six days per week, nine hours per day, with Sundays off. This schedule was retained for the duration of the war, although there were often many people working on Sundays as well.

To effectively use the expanded work force, some changes in organization were necessary, mainly in the Production Division. As before the war, the Commandant of the Navy Yard was in charge. When the war began Rear Admiral W. H. Allen was commandant; in June of 1942 he was relieved by Rear Admiral W. A. Glassford who was replaced by Rear Admiral Jules James the next year. These men also served as Commandants of the Sixth Naval District. In September of 1942, Sixth Naval District headquarters was moved to the Fort Sumter Hotel in downtown Charleston until near the end of the war.

Directly under the Yard Commandant was the Industrial Manager, a Navy captain. When the war started there were six production shops; during the war years five additional shops were created. The first was the Electric Shop, which became a separate entity in July of 1940. A year later the Central Tool Shop was established. In 1943, the Boiler Shop was set up as a separate shop as was the Rigger and Laborer Shop. The Paint Shop was established in 1945.

Looking across the Cooper River to the yard in July of 1941. The Ashley River can be seen at the upper left.

The yard in July of 1941. The lack of development of the North Area is evident — a few years later, that would be changed as housing for yard workers sprang up all over.

EXPANDED FACILITIES

To accommodate the huge increases in the yard workload, new facilities had to be built, despite the many improvements that had been made by the federal relief program in the years before the war.

The biggest single project was Dry Dock 2, completed in April of 1942 at a cost of some $3,000,000. The dock was constructed for the purpose of building two destroyers at a time; it was never used for ship construction, however, because it was urgently needed for repair and conversion work throughout the war.

A total of four new shop buildings were completed in the early years of the war. Two new piers, now designated F and G, were constructed. Roads were built and new crane tracks laid. To provide more room for storage of material, 196 acres of land were purchased on the north and west boundaries of the yard.

These improvements enabled the yard to accommodate the expanded workload in every area save one — building destroyer escorts in a crash program assigned to the yard in January of 1942. For that, a new shipyard was necessary. And one was built in an amazingly short time. The story of how this was done is told elsewhere in this chapter.

Silver-plated casings such as this contained the traditional champagne bottle used in launching ceremonies.

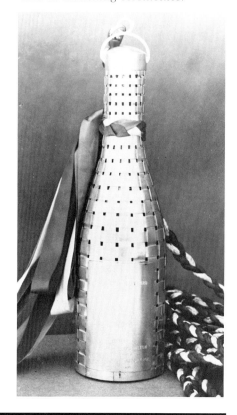

BUILDING SHIPS

From August of 1939 until the surrender of Japan six years later, the Navy Yard built a total of 216 vessels. These ranged from yard tugboats and floating derricks to a huge destroyer tender. Many were warships — destroyers and destroyer escorts. Nine were fast troop transports, based on the DE hull. The rest were landing craft for the invasions of Europe and North Africa and for island hopping in the vast Pacific.

When Germany invaded Poland, the yard was engaged in the biggest new construction program in its history. Most of the effort was in building destroyers. The *Roe* (DD-418) was being fitted out and two more like her were on the ways.

Courtesy S. F. Fennessy.

The launching tags for some Charleston-built destroyers. These were used to identify members of the launching crew.

VESSELS BUILT AT THE YARD

1939-1945

Destroyers	20
Destroyer escorts	17
Fast troop transports	9
Tank landing ships	8
Medium landing ships	92
Medium landing ships (rocket)	24
Landing craft-control	24
Yard tugs	5
Seaplane wrecking derricks	15
Car float	1
Destroyer tender	1
Total	216

In the next two years before Pearl Harbor, the yard continued to concentrate on destroyer construction. After America formally entered the war the emphasis turned to destroyer escorts to protect the convoys which were ferrying troops and huge amounts of war materials to Europe. Then in the summer of 1942 the yard laid the keels on its first landing craft, one of a series of eight tank landing ships or LSTs. These were good-sized ocean-going ships, each displacing 1,490 tons.

Construction methods were somewhat different from those employed on destroyers. Much of the work was subcontracted and the vessels prefabricated to a great extent. The LSTs were followed by a series of ninety-two LSMs, medium-size landing ships. Some of these vessels were built in as little as forty-nine days. Another type landing craft built by the yard was the LCC. Twenty-four of these fifty-six-foot-long vessels were built and fitted with the latest sonar and communications gear.

After experience with landing craft in the Pacific the Navy saw the advantage of heavily arming the vessels. Rocket launchers were installed and the craft designated LSM(R)s. The Navy Yard built twenty-four of these vessels, launching the last one in February of 1945.

The last vessels built by the yard were two destroyer tenders. The first was the *Tidewater* (AD-31) which slid into the Cooper River on 30 June 1945. The keel for the *Bryce Canyon* (AD-36) was laid a week later but she was not completed until years after the war.

REPAIR AND CONVERSION WORK

When the war began in Europe, the yard was doing little repair and conversion work. Nearly all of the production work force was engaged in building destroyers. The repair workload gradually increased; by the time of Pearl Harbor some 2,000 workmen were engaged in overhaul and repair operations.

After America formally went to war, repair of ships fighting in the conflict became top priority. Getting them back to sea as soon as humanly possible was vital to the war effort. Dry Dock 1 was kept continuously busy. Dry Dock 2, completed in early 1942, could never be used for its intended purpose of building destroyers because it was urgently needed for ship repair.

Nor were the two dry docks enough. Several small floating dry docks were pressed into service. Barges were used to support vessels being repaired. Some vessels were lifted by bow or stern to work on the underwater hull. Others were inclined to the maximum safe list, much as wooden ships had been heaved down or careened at the state navy yards during the American Revolution.

The warships repaired included cruisers, destroyers, and destroyer escorts. Hospital ships, gunboats, patrol craft, and Coast Guard cutters came to the yard for overhaul. Vessels were converted and modified and new armaments were installed. Not only naval vessels were repaired, but also merchant ships. The SS *Stanvac Melborne* entered the yard with a huge hole ripped in her side by a U-boat torpedo.

Many British vessels were repaired at the yard. The *Uganda*, a British cruiser torpedoed near Gibraltar, was towed into the Navy Yard with many dead sealed in her hull. Canadian, Dutch, Free French, Greek, Norwegian, Colombian, and Peruvian ships were also repaired.

The biggest repair job done by the yard during the war was on the French-manned destroyer escort *Sengalais*. She had been split in two in a battle with a German U-boat. The entire stern of the vessel from just aft of the stack was sunk, while the forward section of the vessel miraculously remained afloat. Even as the stern section settled under the sea, the guns of the *Sengalais* blazed away at the U-boat, which itself was sunk in the battle.

The truncated vessel, with a sinking U-boat painted on her stack, was towed to Charleston. The yard constructed an entire stern section in one of the building docks alongside two LSMs. The new stern was carefully joined to the undamaged part of the vessel and the two sections welded together, making the *Sengalais* a whole ship again.

The last major repair job accomplished by the Navy Yard during the war was on the light cruiser *Reno*. On 3 November 1944, the *Reno* had been heavily damaged by a torpedo from a Japanese plane which ripped a twenty-foot by sixty-foot hole in her side. After temporary repairs she arrived in Charleston the next March. The yard rebuilt much of the vessel, using more than 500 tons of new structural steel in the process.

Dry Dock 2, shown here in May of 1942, was constructed to build destroyers. It never was used for this purpose because it was needed for repair and overhaul work.

The Men of The Yard

R. McC. FIGG
Master Molder

J. P. KANE
Master Shipfitter

J. T. FEARING
Master Machinist

Captain C. J. Harter, Yard Supply Officer (right) huddles to keep warm while Rear Admiral Jules James, the Yard Commandant, seems to be telling a fish story. The occasion was the official opening of the new yard cold storage plant on 20 May 1943.

PRODUCTION DIVISION
MASTER MECHANICS

In 1940, these men were in charge of the production shops at the yard.

J. E. DAWSON
Master Joiner & Rigger

W. B. R. MITCHELL
Master Electrician

A. OLDMIXON
Master Pipefitter

W. B. HOOD
Master Sheet Metal Worker

On the eve of the Second World War, the shipfitters formed one of the key yard trades for the expanding shipbuilding program. These were the supervisors of the Shipfitters Shop in 1940. Sitting, left to right: Foreman P. L. Dickinson; Master J. P. Kane. First row, left to right: Gerald Sigwald, quarterman driller; James Murphy, S. T. Garman, quarterman shipfitters; H. J. Fortune, S. H. Hanley, quarterman chipper and caulkers; C. W. Wilkerson, T. F. Sinclair, quarterman shipfitters; W. B. Cox, chief quarterman shipfitter; J. B. Hughes, chief quarterman loftsman; A. B. Flynn, chief quarterman chipper and caulker; C. H. Townsend, chief quarterman shipfitter; J. Goree, R. Archambault, C. A. Allison, D. J. Bullock, W. B. Fisher, quarterman shipfitters; C. O. Wilson, quarterman gas cutter and burner. Second row, left to right: A. Borkoski, leadingman chipper and caulker; T. O. Cammer, leadingman anglesmith; C. A. Melvin, C. Ott, E. Fennessy, J. Crow, A. Almers, T. Piasczyc, H. Knight, W. Logan, leadingman shipfitters; W. Poplin, W. Douglas, J. Massalon, gas cutter and burners; T. Rauth, W. Ketchum, chipper and caulkers; A. Buero, leadingman shipfitter. Third row, left to right: O. J. Marchant, leadingman driller; W. J. Voight, leadingman chipper and calker; L. C. Brown, E. H. Kornahrens, A. P. Mangano, leadingman shipfitters; E. Wan Delken, leadingman driller; W. A. DeJean, R. G. Crowley, B. McBell, W. H. Crawford, leadingman shipfitters; I. Rhodes, leadingman driller; J. W. Roumillat, chipper and calker; T. MacPherson, leadingman loftsman; D. J. Miller, leadingman shipfitter; H. B. Croft, leadingman driller.

The supervisors of the Pipe Shop in 1941. First row, left to right: Charles T. Woodley, leadingman pipefitter; Walter A. Blois, leadingman plumber; Melville C. Wilson, leadingman pipefitter; Clarence G. Thompson, quarterman coppersmith; Miner G. Haney, quarterman pipecoverer and insulator; Michael J. Inabinet, quarterman plumber; William T. Ryan, Jr., chief quarterman plumber and pipefitter; Jewell V. Morris, Christopher H. A. Matthews, quarterman pipefitter; Clarence D. Puckhaber, quarterman plumber; Ernest G. Duncan, Sr., leadingman plumber; George O. Baker, William B. Solyom, Henry G. Smith, leadingman pipefitters. Back row, left to right: Campy Williams, Robert W. Escoffier, leadingman pipecoverers and insulators; Charles E. Arnold, leadingman pipefitter; Wallace Crawford, leadingman pipecoverer and insulator; William B. Osborne, leadingman pipefitter; Edward Bates, pipecoverer and insulator; Thomas J. Weeks, leadingman pipefitter; Robert F. McDougall, leadingman coppersmith; John H. Webber, Albert J. Doneely, leadingman plumbers; Fred M. Hunt, leadingman pipefitter; John R. Malone, leadingman coppersmith; Benjamin B. Rodgers, Oscar D. Rose, leadingman pipefitters. Absent when picture was taken: Adrian Oldmixon, master plumber and pipefitter; James W. Wilson, Alex F. Barbrey, quarterman pipefitters; Gilbert H. Kent, leadingman pipefitter; John H. Darby, leadingman plumber.

Courtesy A. A. Ilderton.

The supervisors in charge of building ways and building dock activities in 1943. Left to right: C. M. Wilkerson, chief quarterman shipfitter, inside: C. H. Townsend, foreman shipfitter in charge of all X11 activities on Building Ways and in Building Docks; A. A. Ilderton, quarterman welder; T. R. Bolchoz, Jr. chief quarterman welder; J. B. Hughes, foreman mold loft man; P. L. Dickinson, foreman shipfitter assistant to master shipfitter; A. Flynn, foreman shipper and caulker; T. Doran, quarterman shipfitter; W. J. Tucker, chief quarterman shipwright; W. A. Ankerson, quarterman shipwright; W. D. Bateman, chief quarterman rigger; P. Danielson, quarterman rigger.

Shortly after Pearl Harbor, the Industrial Department's Rifle Security Squad was organized to augment the yard police force in an emergency such as an air raid. There were three divisions, one for each shift. These photographs were taken in October of 1942 in front of Building 43.

As the yard workforce dramatically increased, training took on added importance. These men formed the staff of the Apprentice School in 1940. On the front row, left to right: Raymond L. Denaux, instructor; Eugene C. Figg, senior apprentice supervisor; and Albert P. Rollins, instructor. On the back row, left to right: Francis H. Burnett, William M. Miller, Jr., John G. Morrison, and Allison Siegling, instructors. Not in the picture was Thomas S. Reid, instructor.

In May of 1944, joiner O. C. Eaddy demonstrates a new fiberglass knife he and his three coworkers designed to make better-fitting ship's insulation pieces. From the left are Edgar P. Robinson, James B. Tadlock, Eaddy and Willie E. Stone.

One of many workers who left to fight and later came back was Hobson J. Varnadoe of the Sheet Metal Shop. He spent twenty-two months in the South Pacific before stopping a hunk of shrapnel. The Smoaks, S. C. resident returned to his job at the yard shortly after his medical discharge. His father, two brothers, and a sister also worked at the yard.

Although many brought their own lunches, feeding the huge numbers of Navy Yard workers was a massive undertaking. Here yard workers are served in the cafeteria main dining room in August of 1944.

In the spring of 1940 as the yard workforce increased by leaps and bounds, a severe housing shortage developed in the North Area. The United States Housing Authority had three apartment projects constructed to house the new yard workers. The first to be completed in March of 1941 was known as Tom McMillan Homes. These buildings were eventually torn down to make room for the Naval Regional Medical Center.

Another of the apartment projects was Ben Tillman Homes. Four hundred units were completed in August of 1941 and quickly occupied. There were long waiting lists for the prestigious new apartments.

The third project was George Legare Homes, finished also in August of 1941. Together, the three complexes provided some 1,236 modern apartments for yard workers, almost tripling the available housing in the North Area. Each of the three projects was named for an important congressional supporter of the Navy Yard.

The Reynolds Avenue gate in January of 1941.

Looking west from the power plant in July of 1942. The building in the left background is Eliza Lucas Hall, once one of the finest YWCAs in the nation. Eliza Lucas Hall was destroyed by fire in 1966.

Iron and steel were precious during the Second World War — enough so that this strange contraption, a magnetic sweeper, was used at the yard to pick up small pieces of the ferrous metals.

This Navy Yard float, featuring a miniature replica of the Power House, was one of several entered in local parades by the yard in the 1940s.

This little tram, a refugee from the New York World's Fair, was used to haul workers around the yard during the war.

The Destroyers

In a five-year period, from 1938 to 1943, the yard launched twenty new destroyers into the Cooper River. They were fast, well-armed, multi-purpose ships, lean and hard and all business. The first was the *Sterett* (DD-407). The last one was the *Bryant* (DD-665), commissioned on 4 December 1943.

Typical of the "tin cans" was the *Tillman* (DD-641), the second destroyer named for Pitchfork Ben, the yard's early benefactor. The destroyer was 348 feet long with a beam of thirty-six feet and a displacement of 1,630 tons. She carried four five-inch guns, four 1.1-inch guns, five twenty-millimeter anti-aircraft cannons and five torpedo tubes. Steaming at full speed she could make 37.4 knots, still very fast by the standards of today.

World War II destroyers were multi-threat warships, able to take on an enemy on the shore, on the sea, in the air, or in ocean depths. The Charleston vessels served all over the world, in the freezing waters of the north Atlantic, in the English Channel, in the Mediterranean, in the Pacific. They did everything that the Navy needed done, from convoy duty, to bombarding enemy shore positions, to protecting their carriers from Japanese Zeros, to hauling supplies to the embattled Pacific islands.

The life at sea was hard and filled with danger. Five of the twenty never came home from the war. But the tough little ships and others like them did the job. They were, in the words of one admiral, "the fightingest things afloat."

On 17 July 1939, the keel was laid for the Grayson (DD-435). She was named for Rear Admiral Cary T. Grayson, a Navy doctor who was President Wilson's personal physician during the First World War.

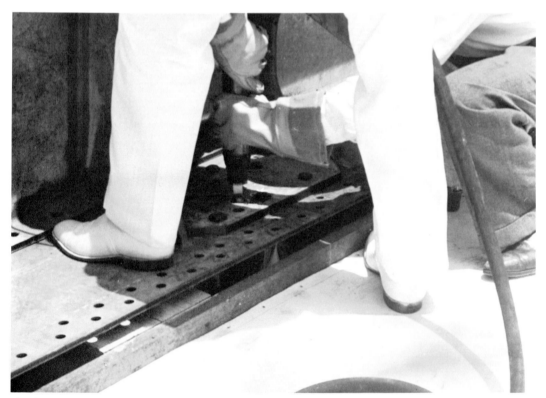

The first rivet is driven in the keel of the Grayson, a traditional part of the keel-laying ceremony.

U.S.S. GRAYSON
DESTROYER
NAMED FOR
REAR ADMIRAL CAREY TRAVERS GRAYSON, U.S.N.
BUILT BY THE NAVY YARD CHARLESTON, S.C.

AUTHORIZED	JULY. 23, 1938
KEEL LAID	JULY. 17, 1939
LAUNCHED	AUG. 7, 1940
FIRST COMMISSIONED	FEB. 14, 1941

On 8 September 1941, the Hobson (DD-464) was christened at the yard by Mrs. Richard P. Hobson.

In March of 1942, the Hobson slowly steams up the Cooper River. On the night of 26 April 1952, Hobson was taking part in a training exercise in the Atlantic when she crossed in front of the carrier Wasp and the two collided. Hobson broke in two and sank with a loss of 176 hands in one of the Navy's worst peacetime disasters.

On 28 October 1941, the bow section of the second Tillman (DD-641) was fitted to the forward section of the vessel on the building ways.

John D. Jennings, Chairman of the Navy Yard Central Shop Committee, presents a gift to Mrs. Mary Middleton Lee just before the launching of the destroyer named for her grandfather, Lieutenant Ralph Izard, USN. The Izard family is an old Charleston family.

The crew of the Ingraham (DD-444) proudly assembled for this formal portrait just before the new vessel's commissioning in June of 1941. Less than a year later, the vessel was sunk in a collision with an oil tanker in a heavy fog off the coast of Nova Scotia. Only eleven of her crew members survived.

The destroyer Bell (DD-587) steams down the Cooper River in March of 1943. She saw action in many battles in the Pacific, earning twelve battle stars for her participation in the war.

With her war paint in place, the Bryant passes under the Cooper River bridge headed for sea in March of 1944. She was the last of twenty destroyers built by the Navy Yard during the war.

Vessel	Fate
Ingraham, DD 444	Sunk in collision, 1942
Beatty, DD 641	Sunk by torpedo, 1943
Corry, DD 463	Sunk by mine, 1944
Pringle, DD 477	Sunk by kamikazi, 1944
Twiggs, DD 591	Sunk by torpedo and kamikazi, 1945
Hobson, DD 464	Sunk in collision, 1952

Of twenty Charleston-built destroyers constructed during World War II, five were lost at sea during the war. In addition, two Charleston-built LSTs and five LSMs were sunk.

A Charleston Destroyer Goes To War

The USS *Grayson* (DD-435) saw more action in World War II than any other Charleston-built vessel. She went to sea a few months before Pearl Harbor. Before the war was over she had earned thirteen battle stars for missions ranging from convoy duty in the icy North Atlantic to escorting the carrier *Enterprise* in bloody battles off Guadalcanal.

The following account of the "*G*" in action in the South Pacific is taken from the book *Condition Red — Destroyer Action in the South Pacific* written in 1943 by Frederick J. Bell. Commander Bell was the skipper of the *Grayson*. The action took place on 24 August 1942 as the destroyer was doing her best to protect the *Enterprise*.

Early on this August forenoon we received a reconnaissance report that at least one Japanese carrier was within three hundred miles; a stone's throw as distances are measured in the Pacific and as sea battles are waged in their opening phase. With her was the usual guard of destroyers and cruisers. Our own planes took off immediately and for hours they had been hammering the enemy Task Force. From fragments of information during the day we gathered that one Japanese carrier had been sunk, and a second set on fire. It was time now, for our air group to return. They had ex-

hausted their ammunition and were so nearly out of gas that they would have to follow a direct course in rejoining, thereby showing the way to any Japanese air groups that might still be available to attack. There were too few ships in our screen to spare any of us as a surface striking force. It would be an anti-aircraft engagement. From the carrier our admiral signaled: "Prepare to repel air attack." We gathered close around our Flat Top in readiness for action.

Within the steel walls of the G, three hundred officers and men took a last-minute inventory of their tools of war. In the wardroom the surgeon opened out his equipment on the officers' dining table. On the bulkhead he hung up a square of canvas fitted with pockets and pouches for kits of medical hardware. Along the leather seats of the transoms he laid his bottles, to cushion them against the shattering concussion of gunfire. In destroyers there are no hospital beds or isolation wards. The medical officer dispenses from a cubicle of a sick bay, and in action he uses the wardroom or a crews' compartment for his knotting and splicing. There is duplicate equipment aft, under the charge of a chief pharmacist's mate, and there are bags and boxes of dressings, anti-burn solutions and minor medical aids at all battle stations.

Across from the radio shack, in the cramped spaces of the coding room, the Communication Officer passed a lashing through the grommets of a sea bag and tied it securely. Stuffed with secret books, weighted with fire brick to insure sinking, it would be thrown over the

The Grayson steams through Charleston Harbor on 17 April 1941, two months after her commissioning.

side if the ship had to be abandoned through fire or other cause.

Far below, in the intense heat of their oil-scented, methodical world of steam and light and harnessed power, the engineers cracked their valves wide open and the turbines sang in a higher key.

In all lower deck compartments there were wooden shores and an assortment of plugs and wedges of various sizes that could be used as leak stoppers in a hurry, unless the hole in the side should be so large that the entire compartment would have to be blocked off.

The men of the repair parties buckled on their helmets, strapped tool belts around their waists, inspected the valves of rescue masks and slipped their hands into asbestos mittens. Theirs was a waiting game — until the ship was hit. Then they fought fire and the noxious gases of explosion; struggled against the inrush of water in flooding compartments; worked to keep their ship afloat and on an even keel.

Everyone wore a steel helmet. The men topside were bundled in life jackets. Those belowdecks, in the fierce heat and close confinement of narrow steel passages, kept them ready for use.

Unnecessary electric power and all water systems were closed off to decrease possible sources of fire and flooding. At every gun, on the bridge and in the fire rooms, wherever men were stationed, fresh drinking water was provided, for use during lulls in the action when men have time to notice the intense thirst that battle brings.

These details were checked almost subconsciously, but actually there was little to be attended to when the general alarm sounded — other than closing off systems and doors, for all the preliminaries to action were part of our normal wartime cruising routine. We were ready at any time to open fire with half the battery instantly. Within two and a half minutes from the time the order was given to "go to general quarters," all hands were on station, the entire battery was manned, and the ship was in the prescribed Material Condition that gave maximum internal protection against the spread of damage.

Long before the first attacking planes appeared, the ships of the screen had formed a wall around the carrier, their guns pointed skyward. Aboard the G the events leading up to the action took place hurriedly.

The first group of attackers to get safely clear of the carrier came close aboard the G after leveling off from their dives. The pull out slowed them down in so great a contrast between their plummeting dives and the straightaway recovery that they seemed to drift along our side and only a few feet above us. They did not have retractable landing gear. I remembered our machine-gun officer's instructions to his crews — "If the ducks have feet, they're enemy." These carrier-based dive bomber ducks had feet — wheels with streamlined hoods that projected beneath the dirty slate-gray fuselage.

The first plane cut over our quarter from starboard to port, less than two hundred feet above our decks. The pilot rolled slightly toward us. In the after cockpit the gunner leaned out and thumbed his nose. Braced against the straps of his 20-mm gun, seaman Robert Otto let the fingers of his left hand slide along the trigger. By the time the Jap struck the water Otto was firing on a new target.

The Grayson *and a sister-ship lie in Seeadler Harbor in the Admiralty Islands, circa 1944. The* Grayson *was the most decorated of Charleston-built destroyers during World War II, earning thirteen battle stars.*

At 1713, carrier hit by a bomb on starboard quarter. There was a dense cloud of gray-white smoke, followed almost immediately by flame.

On the bridge of the G a signalman said "Jesus, that's got her." We looked aft and we thought he was right. Forward of the island the carrier was undamaged; her guns firing as rapidly as ever. Abaft the island there was nothing but smoke, and on the quarter, red tongues of flame shot into the air. We knew that her planes had sunk one Japanese carrier earlier today and damaged another. It looked, now, as if we were to pay a price for our victory.

A dive bomber dropped down, overshot the carrier, and loosed his bomb by the side of the G. The ocean soared upward and fell on our deck. Splinters of steel ripped into the hull. The starboard machine guns checked fire. At this moment another plane came out of his dive and droned past us at bare flying speed. It was duck soup for the machine guns. We could have hit him with a rock. But the guns were not on him. The crews, wiping the water from their faces, startled by the bomb, did not see the target. All except one man. Chief Gunner's Mate William C. Hoppers, the fattest man in the crew of the G, was in charge of the after machine-gun battery. His guns already had accounted for two planes. This third one was easy — but there was no activity along the starboard side. Hoppers shouted at the gun crews. His voice was lost in the noise of battle. He reached down, pulled off his shoes and threw them at the back of the nearest gun captain. It was a bull's eye. The man turned; Hoppers pointed; the gun resumed fire, and the Japanese plane, flames licking its wings, tumbled into the sea.

Forward in the ship, in the lower handling room far below No. 2 gun, someone dropped a shell from a height of several feet. The petty officer in charge beckoned to a seaman. "Run that shell topside and heave it over the side," he ordered. The seaman picked up the hundred-pound projectile and commenced the climb to the upper decks, carefully closing and dogging the doors and hatches behind him. Just as a bomb exploded he arrived on the forecastle. Back down the ladders he went, through compartments, passages and handling room, still remembering to secure the doors and hatches. "Jeez," he said, "just as I got to the forecastle the damndest biggest bomb you ever saw blew up alongside!" He was eager to tell more, but his shipmates would have none of it, for under his arm he still clutched the defective shell that might explode of itself at any moment. "To hell with the bomb!" shouted the P.O. "Get that shell out of here!" So up the seaman climbed again, closing the doors and hatches carefully behind him. And this time he got rid of the shell.

Later the crew talked of how "the Captain saved the ship by putting the rudder hard over so the bomb didn't hit." The truth of the matter was that the Captain put the rudder hard over to avoid collision with something a darned sight bigger than the G, and while he saw the near-miss out of the corner of his eye, it seemed at the time to be by far the lesser of the two evils. If the crew chose to believe that anything other than good luck was responsible for our being able to duck a five-hundred-pound bomb I saw no reason to argue the point.

On 16 October 1945, the G returned home to Charleston, battlescarred and proud. Eleven days later on Navy Day, over 5,000 Charlestonians boarded the vessel to pay tribute to the brave men who had served their country with such honor.

On Navy Day in 1945, over 5,000 Charlestonians went on board the Grayson to pay their respects to the battle-weary vessel and her brave crew. The destroyer was one of many ships open for inspection at the Navy Yard that day.

The yard installed many five-inch guns like this on auxiliary vessels during the war. Once one was fired by accident, the shell fortunately landing in the marsh across the Cooper River.

In the spring of 1942, two trainees of the Navy Yard diving class get ready to enter the muddy waters of the Cooper River.

In March of 1945, the new stern for the destroyer escort Sengalais is ready to be fitted and welded in place. The Free-French vessel had been split in two by a torpedo just aft of her stack. The forward half of the ship was towed to Charleston where the yard built a new stern section in a building dock beside two LSMs. This was the only time the yard built "one-half a ship."

The corvette HMS Nasturtium was one of many British vessels repaired at the yard during the war.

Hull plates of the merchant ship SS Stanvac Melborne were ripped apart by the blast of a U-boat torpedo. Many damaged ships were repaired in the yard during the war.

A repaired propeller from a destroyer awaits transport to the waterfront.

On a rainy day in April of 1943, eight coastal transport vessels were in Dry Dock 2 for repairs.

On 10 May 1942, arrival of thirty-three surviving crew members of a German U-boat caused a stir at the yard. The submarine, U-352, had been sunk off Beaufort, N. C. by the U. S. Coast Guard cutter Icarus the evening before. Here, the German prisoners, guarded by U. S. Marines, line up on Pier 317 (now Pier F) as they leave the Icarus.

National Archives.

When U-352 left St. Nazaire, France in April of 1942 on her second war patrol, the members of the crew hardly expected to end up eating southern fried chicken at the Charleston Navy Yard a month later. The man on the left is Kapitanleutnant Hellmut Rathke, the commanding officer.

National Archives.

The prisoners march through the yard under guard just south of where the fire station now stands. The average age of the members of the crew was twenty-two. Twelve of the crew perished in the sinking and another died aboard the Icarus.

National Archives.

On 6 September 1985, three former crew members of U-352 visited the yard in an historic reunion. Standing where they were photographed forty-three years earlier (above), from left are Kurt Krueger, Lothar Wessoly and Heinz Richter. On the right is Colonel Sam Smith, USMC (retired). As a young lieutenant, Smith was in charge of the prisoners while they were at the yard.

The Destroyer Escort Program And The South Yard

A month after Pearl Harbor, in early January of 1942, the yard received word from the Bureau of Ships to start building destroyer escorts. Barely a week later, a contract had been awarded for twenty of the vessels. The first was to be completed by 1 September 1943 — the last, eight months later.

Such a program was typical of the wartime shipbuilding effort. But to the Navy Yard it was complicated by a hard fact: there were no facilities or equipment to build the vessels. Everything was tied up in existing programs to build destroyers and other vessels and to repair ships fighting in the war. So before construction of the destroyer escorts could begin, a new shipyard had to be built. How this was done is a splendid example of American determination and ingenuity as the nation geared up for war following the humiliation of Pearl Harbor.

The initial discussions among yard managers to decide what would be needed to build the DEs took place on 10 January 1942, shortly after the first telephone calls from Washington. Three weeks later, a study of construction methods used by other yards had been completed and a layout of the required facilities sent to BUSHIPS for approval. On 23 February, the Chief of Naval Operations and the Secretary of the Navy endorsed the

project in the amount of $7,197,000. By that time, the yard had already negotiated contracts with Daniels Construction Company and Southeastern Construction Company to build the new yard. Less than two months from the time the yard learned it was to build destroyer escorts, construction work was ready to start on the new facilities.

The facilities were built where the Coast Guard Airfield was located, south of the torpedo warehouse, Building 101. They amounted to a complete separate shipyard, which became known as the South Yard. The vessels were to be built, two at a time, in each of two small shipbuilding dry docks. Eight new shop buildings were constructed, most with elaborate wooden truss structures to save the precious steel for ships. Pier J was built, Building 79 enlarged and new crane and railroad tracks laid.

As construction work proceeded, the destroyer escort program took on greater urgency. In August construction of twenty-three more DEs was assigned to the yard. Two months later, the schedule for building the ships was stepped up to a rate of forty-eight per year.

The first two vessels were laid down even before the building docks were finished. These were the *Manning* (DE-199) and the *Nevendorf* (DE-200), whose keels were laid in Dry Dock 3 on

In 1938 the emergency landing strip south of the yard was turned into a Coast Guard airfield. The building in the foreground is Building 101, the torpedo warehouse. To the left is Building 590A — then used as a barracks for the Coast Guard Air Station. In 1942, the air field was dismantled to make room for the buildings of the South Yard.

15 February 1943 before the dock pumps were installed. Three and one-half months later, the two vessels were launched by flooding the dock and moved to piers for fitting out. The day after the launch, the construction of thirty-six more DEs was assigned to the yard.

Not long afterwards, however, the need for landing craft became an overriding priority for the Navy. The DE program was cut back as a result. In all, the yard built seventeen of the vessels and completed nine more in a modified version as fast troop transports.

The heavy yard workload at the time made subcontracting much of the work on the vessels a necessity. Twenty-two different contractors were involved with building parts of the ships. The last of the series, the *Upham* (APD-99) was launched in March of 1944.

On 1 January 1943, Dry Dock 3 was nearing completion. In the background can be seen some of the shop buildings of the South Yard.

The shop buildings of the South Yard were constructed using elaborate wooden frames to save the precious steel for shipbuilding.

In May of 1943, destroyer escorts were being built in Dry Dock 3 even before the dock was completed.

Some of the destroyer escorts were constructed on the building ways. Here, the James E. Craig (DE-201) and the Eichenberger (DE-202) are ready for launching.

The crew of the Liddle (DE-206) stands at attention as the commissioning ceremony begins on 6 December 1943. In all, the yard built seventeen destroyer escorts.

The Dickerson (APD-21) in the Cooper River. The yard converted the old four-stack destroyer into a fast troop transport in 1943.

PRODUCE TO WIN!

Vol. III   CHARLESTON NAVY YARD, S. C., NOVEMBER 24, 1944   No. 17

5TH "E" AWARD
WON BY CNY EMPLOYEES

★ ★

Tender's Keel Will Be Laid Monday At CNY

★ ★

Film Star Janet Blair Will Help Launch Big Bond Drive At C.N.Y.

—All Stories, Page 1-A

★ BUY BONDS ★
SOCK THOSE 'SONS OF HEAVEN' FROM DECEMBER ONE TO SEVEN

PEARL HARBOR DAY

CNY MALES WILL CELEBRATE EYE DAY Monday when lovely Janet Blair of the screen comes to the Yard to help launch the Yard's War Bond drive.

The aim of the yard newspaper of the World War II era was clearly evident in its title. It kept yard workers up-to-date on all the latest developments, at least those permitted by the wartime security restrictions.

Many shops honored their workers who went to war with wooden plaques like this one. In all, 4,047 Navy Yard workers joined the armed services during the Second World War.

On 21 November 1942, the keel of LST-360 was laid. She was the last of the eight big tank landing ships built by the yard. Three arcs were struck simultaneously by (from left) F. G. Meitzler, leadingman electrician; L. E. Haistens, quarterman patternmaker; and J. L. Madden, chief quarterman joiner, each assisted by his wife, as Captain A. M. Penn, the Navy Yard Industrial Manager, looks on.

LST-357 was launched from the building ways on 14 December 1942.

Just after the launching, tugs push the tank landing ship to a pier for fitting out. The vessel saw her first combat on the beaches of North Africa. She later participated in the invasions of Sicily, Salerno, and Normandy. During the Normandy invasion she made more than forty trips between England and France, delivering tanks, equipment, and troops and returning with Allied casualties and German prisoners.

"Not once did the 357 ever fail us in an emergency. She was also the fastest LST in Europe, and I'd be willing to bet money on it. I know she could out-run every LST we ever came across. The men and women of the Charleston Navy Yard who built the 357 really have a right to be proud of old 'Palermo Pete.' "

Lieutenant (jg) L. M. Stern,
XO LST 357

In June of 1945, LST-357 became the first Charleston-built tank landing ship to return from combat. She was known as "Palermo Pete" by her crew. This name came from the vessel's mascot, a stuffed stork some of the sailors picked up in Palermo.

NAVY ASKS CNY
TO DOUBLE QUOTA OF CRAFT
FOR INVASION!

Vol. II   CHARLESTON NAVY YARD, S. C., MAY 5, 1944   No. 40

STORY ON PAGE 1-A

The Navy Yard launched fifty-eight LSMs and LSM(R)s in the last six months of 1944.

LSM 152 steams down the Cooper River in July of 1944.

LSM 152 cruises in the Cooper River on 25 July 1944, three days after she was commissioned. The yard completed the vessel in sixty-five days; some LSMs were built in as little as forty-nine days.

Two medium landing ships, LSM-126 and LSM-127, were launched at the Navy Yard on 15 March 1944. These were the first two of ninety-two such vessels built by the yard.

Yard workmen prepare equipment for a LSM(R) in the shop in February of 1945.

PRODUCE TO WIN!

Vol. III   CHARLESTON NAVY YARD, S. C., JANUARY 12, 1945   No. 24

The last twenty-four landing vessels built by the yard were LSM(R)s, the first of which was launched in September of 1944. Not until four months later did the yard newspaper announce that these vessels were being constructed by yard workers.

Now It Can Be Told! CNY Builds
ROCKET SHIPS

Three Charleston-built LSM(R)s bombard Pokishi Shinia, near Okinawa, in March of 1945. With hundreds of rockets, these little vessels each carried 2½ times the firepower of a broadside from the battleship New Jersey.

The Women

Mattie Nettles was a great-grandmother. Her three sons all worked at the Navy Yard, as well as her grandson, Walter Idlerton. In 1944, she lived alone in her house in Summerville, "just me and the Lord," she would say.

Each morning, except for Sundays, she got up at four o'clock. After tidying up her house, she put on her slacks, wrapped a turban around her white hair and packed her lunch just in time to catch the five-thirty bus to Charleston.

By seven o'clock, Mattie was at work. Her job, however, was a lot different from those which women traditionally did in the Lowcountry. Mattie was a shipfitter at the Navy Yard.

She worked at a big machine in the Shipfitter Shop, pressing out steel plates to be used in landing craft and other vessels being built and repaired by the yard. Grandma Nettles, as she was called,

was known as a careful and conscientious worker. One day she asked for a day off and got her supervisor's permission. But when the whistle blew the next morning she was back at her job at the big steel press. She explained that, "I just got to thinking that if all those boys out there needed things, it wasn't going to be me that held them up, as long as I can help it."

Mattie was one of thousands of women who worked at the yard during the war, doing things that before the war women just didn't do. The first women were employed in the production shops in the spring of 1942. Less than three years later, there were nearly five thousand women at the Navy Yard, most employed in non-traditional occupations.

They did nearly everything. Some were sailmakers — women did nearly all the upholstery work for the ships. More than fifty women worked in the Building 1171 Pipe Shop in the South Yard as insulators. They were automobile mechanics, machinists, welders, gas cutters and burners, policewomen, and even riggers. In June of 1944, more than eighty women worked on the building ways helping turn out landing craft.

They often were hired to replace yard workmen who had joined the armed services. And, like the men, they came from all over. From Ridgeville, from Moncks Corner, from Barnwell, from Anderson and all over the state. From other states such as Georgia, North Carolina, and Tennessee and as far away as Mississippi. Many were housewives who had never been employed before, most with brothers and fathers fighting in the war or working at the yard. Some had worked at the Naval Clothing Factory at the yard during the First World War.

In the beginning, women chosen to go in production shops were designated "mechanical learners." Their first week at the yard was spent in training, watching films, touring the shops, being briefed on what they were to do. At the end of the week they were given tests and interviewed and then assigned to a shop — one of their choice, if possible.

After that they joined the work force, taking their place alongside the men. Many of the women became full-fledged mechanics before the war's end.

Grandma Nettles on the job in the Shipfitter Shop.

Mrs. Corinne Creel of the Joiners Shop worked at the yard during the war.

"Riggerette" Christine Jackson waves nonchalantly from the yardarm of the mast of a destroyer escort in April of 1944. Mrs. Jackson, a Navy wife from Kansas City, specialized in working aloft rigging antenna wire and other gear on masts of ships.

In February of 1944, a group of women workers get ready to ride the Brock (DE-234) down the ways. These seventeen women worked at many different trades, from helper shipfitter and helper rigger to engraver and tool checker.

By February of 1944, the yard has women auto mechanics. The first three were, left to right: Grace Lewis, Mildred Eason and Alma Clark.

Catherine Perry waves from the cab of her locomotive in May of 1944. A former bookkeeper for a Charleston restaurant, she worked as a signal person on the yard diesel locomotive. Before that, she had driven a fork lift at the yard.

Welding instructor Julius Seymour shows nineteen-year-old helper-trainee Arlene Harvey how to handle welding equipment. She was Seymour's 2,000th student since the welding school on the building ways opened at the beginning of the war.

A group of mechanical learners tour the yard in June of 1944 as part of their indoctrination. After a week's training, the women would be assigned to help build landing craft or learn a trade in one of the shops.

Four new Navy Yard policewomen pose for the photographer in February of 1944. Left to right, are: Irene Duncan, Sadie Scurfield, Ruby Hale and Vernie Nettles.

While thousands of women worked in non-traditional occupations, many others such as Pearl Harbour Jenkins were employed in traditional office jobs. Mrs. Jenkins, a clerk in the Planning Section, was featured in Ripley's Believe It or Not because of her name.

In December of 1943, Vyvian Williams left the yard War Production Office to become a Women's Air Force Service Pilot. After seven months of training, she ferried planes and served as a test pilot until the WASP program was disbanded in December of 1944. Shortly thereafter, she returned to the yard where she worked until her retirement in 1970. At the time of her retirement she was head of the Employee Services Division.

While their mothers worked, someone had to take care of the children. These kids are on the playground of the George Legare Nursery School in the summer of 1944.

As Elizabeth Garner pretends to talk to her mom at the Navy Yard, her sister Barbara gets ready to take Raggedy Ann for a stroll. The little girl with the bandaged toe is Saunda Carney. Kay Frances Grantham (right) is obviously bored with the whole thing. George Legare Nursery School, where this photograph was taken, was one of three major kindergartens for children of Navy Yard workers. The others were at Liberty Homes and Liberty Homes Extension.

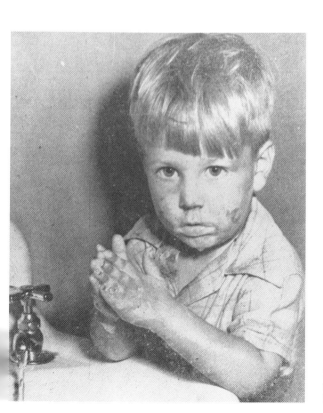

Two-year-old Joe Sanders, Jr. washes up after a hard day at nursery school. His father was a machinist at the Navy Yard. His mother worked in the hull drafting room.

With vessels being launched so frequently, even little girls got in the act. Here Miss Marion Louise Owens prepares to christen the seaplane derrick YSD-34. These craft were designed to salvage wrecked seaplanes.

Courtesy A. A. Ilderton.

On 27 November 1944, the keel for the destroyer tender Tidewater was laid at the yard. Here the first arcs are struck. Assisting Rear Admiral James on the right is Augustus Ilderton, quarterman welder. Eugene Figg of the Apprentice School is standing in the left background.

On 30 June 1945, the destroyer tender Tidewater, the biggest ship the yard had ever built, was launched from the ways. Congressman L. Mendel Rivers was the speaker at the ceremony which was attended by thousands of yard workers.

Special restraints had to be rigged to the stern of the Tidewater to keep her from beaching herself on the opposite shore after the launching. Eight hundred yard workers were required to launch the vessel.

The Medregal (SS-480) was overhauled in a yard floating dry dock in 1952, three weeks ahead of schedule. The yard set a new Navy record by unshipping the vessel in preparation for her snorkle conversion in eight days flat.

6

The Post War Years

Even before World War II ended, work at the yard began to slow down as the Navy cancelled ship construction contracts. Employment dropped rapidly. The workload shifted to preparing surplus ships for layup and disposing of thousands of tons of surplus materials. Then in 1948 one of the key decisions in the yard's history was made when it was designated a submarine yard by the Bureau of Ships. From that time onward, repair and overhaul of submarines made up a major portion of the work of the shipyard.

CHARLESTON NAVAL SHIPYARD

During the war, the naval shore establishment was dramatically expanded. At one point in 1943, there were more than 350,000 people employed at the navy yards. To better manage the shipyards, bases and other shoreside establishments, the Navy made major organizational changes shortly after the war was over.

The United States Naval Base, Charleston, South Carolina was created on 30 November 1945 to integrate the various naval functions at Charleston. The Navy Yard was redesignated the Charleston Naval Shipyard, as one of the components of the new base. The Navy Yard Commandant became the Shipyard Commander. The Commander of the Naval Base took over as Commandant of the Sixth Naval District. In addition to the shipyard, the Naval Base included nine other commands: the naval air station south of the yard, the naval hospital, the marine barracks, the receiving station, the training station, the radio station, the small base on the Ashley River and the ammunition depot up the Cooper River from the yard.

With the new name came a new role for the yard. No longer would the yard build ships, except for completing the *Tidewater* which had been launched a few months before Japan surrendered, and finishing five years later her sistership, the *Bryce Canyon*. The shipyard's new role would be support of the fleet by repairing and overhauling ships, converting them and installing the latest hardware and armaments.

At the end of the war, the United States Navy had an incredible total of some 69,000 vessels ranging from battleships and aircraft carriers to small landing craft and coastal defense vessels. The work of the naval shipyards turned to undoing much of what they had accomplished during wartime: scrapping incomplete vessels, disposing of vast quantities of materials on hand at the yards and decommissioning and putting "in mothballs" ships that were no longer needed.

Nests of decommissioned destroyers lie in the Wando River in April of 1946. That month, the fiftieth ship decommissioned at the yard since the end of the war was added to the group.

At Charleston, the ships began to come in as soon as the war was over. By March of 1946 as many as thirty-five ships at a time were waiting in line to be decommissioned. Many were destroyers, which were laid up in the Wando River in nests of six vessels. In each group, one of the six carried a small crew to maintain the ships. There was not enough space at the piers for all the ships so fifty LSTs and twenty-two LSMs were beached in the north yard for unloading. In all, the yard eventually decommissioned some four hundred vessels. These ships became part of the Atlantic Reserve Fleet.

In 1947, approximately 130 vessels of the "moth-ball" fleet were moved back to the yard at six new piers built at the south end of the shipyard for this purpose. More than one hundred of these vessels were destroyers. The rest were destroyer escorts and other craft and the destroyer tender *Tidewater*.

Another program of the post-war years involved preparations for transfer of American ships to other countries. In 1947, for example, the yard prepared ten ships for transfer to the Turkish Navy. Other vessels were outfitted and turned over to China, Spain, Norway and West Germany.

A SUBMARINE YARD

In April of 1948, Secretary of Navy John L. Sullivan announced that the shipyard would be designated a submarine overhaul yard. The first submarine, the *Conger* (SS-477), arrived for overhaul that August. Shipyard workers had, however, been introduced to submarine overhaul work two years before on a captured German submarine, the U-2513.

U-2513 arrived in Charleston on 12 August 1946. During a six-week period the yard put her in Dry Dock 1 and aligned the propeller shafts, rebuilt part of a fuel oil tank, and did other repairs. The work was complicated by the fact that no plans were available and all the equip-

On 27 August 1948, the Conger arrived at the yard for overhaul. She was the first submarine overhauled here after Charleston was designated a submarine overhaul yard by the Bureau of Ships the previous April.

ment was built in metric sizes. Despite such difficulties, the work was completed on schedule and drew praise from the commanding officer and his superiors and the Bureau of Ships. Not long after she left the yard, President Truman made a deep dive in the vessel off Key West.

Two years later, work on the *Conger* began in the floating dry dock, ARD-15. *Conger* was followed by the *Cubera* (SS-347) in November of 1948 and the *Irex* (SS-482) two months later. Additional submarine overhauls followed at a steady rate, each taking three to four months to accomplish.

A THREAT TO CLOSE THE YARD

Just as the yard's submarine overhaul program was getting underway, the very existence of the shipyard was threatened.

In 1949, as part of President Truman's economy drive, work at the naval shipyards was cut back. Secretary of Defense Louis Johnson issued an order to lay off 70,000 civilian workers at naval installations. A Navy board of admirals recommended closing four naval shipyards: the California yards at Long Beach and San Francisco, the Philadelphia yard and the one at Charleston.

Charlestonians fought to save the yard. The drive was led by Joseph P. Riley of the Chamber of Commerce. A committee of shipyard employees joined the fight. South Carolina Senators Burnet Maybank and Olin D. Johnston and Congressman Lucius Mendel Rivers of the Charleston district carried the battle to Washington and convinced the Secretary of the Navy and the Chief of Naval Operations to keep the yard open. Although the yard wasn't closed, employment was reduced by twenty-eight percent, reaching its post-war low of 4,614 persons in December of 1949.

On 7 November 1950, Congressman L. Mendel Rivers of the First Congressional District of South Carolina made one of his many visits to the shipyard. At his left is Rear Admiral R. W. Hayler, Commandant of the Sixth Naval District. They are standing in front of the bell from the cruiser Charleston at Memorial Square.

Midget brothers Eulie H. David (left) and Eugene S. David, Jr. are congratulated on their return to the shipyard in March of 1951. Both men worked as welders during World War II. Shaking Eulie's hand is Haynes Adams of the Industrial Relations Division. Congratulating his brother Eugene is Corinne Rhodes.

Mendel Rivers, by this time, had become known as an outspoken advocate of a strong national defense. From the time he became a member of the House of Representatives in 1941, he was involved in military matters, first as a member of the Naval Affairs Committee, in later years as Chairman of the Armed Services Committee. Not since Ben Tillman had the shipyard such a powerful friend in Congress. And never in the twentieth century had the military such a strong supporter on Capitol Hill. It was said of Rivers that he had two children — the armed forces and the First Congressional District of South Carolina. The congressman stayed close to his shipyard constituents, often joining yard workers at picnics and barbeques.

THE KOREAN WAR

With the Korean War came a substantial increase in work for the yard. The *Bryce Canyon* was completed. The submarine workload increased; in 1951 the yard overhauled twelve subs, as many as the Philadelphia yard and more than Portsmouth, the other east coast naval shipyard specializing in submarines. In 1950 and 1951, three destroyers were converted to escort vessels, DDEs, by the yard.

Work on the *Bryce Canyon* proceeded without publicity for security reasons in the early months of the Korean War. On 15 September 1950, the big destroyer tender was commissioned, the first new naval vessel completed since the United Nations forces had entered the Korean conflict.

Employment at the yard steadily increased. By 1951, the yard had more than 8,000 workers. Among the new employees were two midgets, the David brothers, who had been hired as welders at the Navy Yard during the Second World War, specializing in working in tight places where others couldn't get. Yard employment reached its post-war high of 9,220 people in July of 1952.

Following the Korean War, the work of the yard continued to be a mixture of submarine overhauls and repair and conversion of surface vessels. Nine Liberty ships were converted to radar station ships and three Victory ships into ocean survey vessels.

The destroyer tender Bryce Canyon, sistership to the Tidewater, was completed early in the Korean War. The big destroyer tender was the last vessel to be built by the yard.

During this period, there was another development that was unsettling to many yard workers. In 1953, the Secretary of the Navy ordered that separate facilities for blacks and whites at the shipyard and other naval installations be eliminated. No longer would there be separate drinking fountains and separate dining rooms. On 19 October 1953, the shipyard cafeteria was desegregated by abolishing the separate dining rooms for blacks and whites. Most white workers stopped eating at the cafeteria and, eventually, a white boycott of the cafeteria developed which lasted for more than three years. The yard was reported by the Associated Press to be the last naval installation in the United States to maintain partial racial segregation.

There had been many black workers at the yard since the early years. In the 1950s, about one worker in four was black. Few held responsible positions, however, until the Navy's affirmative action plans were placed in effect a decade later.

In the 1950s, a great deal of design work was done by the shipyard. In 1958, for example, Charleston was the lead design yard for twenty-six different types of vessels. The yard also performed the design work on many ship conversions completed during the 1950s.

Over the years, several key decisions were made that greatly affected the future of the yard. One was the designation of Charleston as a new construction yard in 1933 that led to the great shipbuilding effort of the Second World War. Perhaps even more important was the Navy's decision in 1948 to make the shipyard a submarine overhaul yard, for in the following years submarines became an increasingly important element of the fleet. Another key decision was that Charleston would become a nuclear shipyard. Although this decision was made by the Bureau of Ships in 1956, it would be the early 1960s before the shipyard really got in the business of working on nuclear-powered submarines.

⚓

The Thornback was overhauled at the yard in 1956. Note the sonar dome just forward of her sail. In the background can be seen the steeple of St. Philip's with the United States Custom House to the right.

The Building 79 Machine Shop ordnance area, circa 1946. Standing in the left foreground is J. T. Fearing, Master Machinist.

In May of 1946, boilermaker Ralph Beard seals a destroyer smokestack with a portable cover he designed himself. Such covers were used on all the decommissioned destroyers laid up in the Wando.

Six nominees for "Miss CNS" of 1948. The winner, Margaret Binnicher, pictured at upper right, got to ride the shipyard float in the Azalea Parade. The other ladies, on the front row from the left, are Peggy Cargill, Helen Mizzell, and Ethelyn Gilbert. On the back row, from the left, are Frances Wallace, Dorothy Monserrat and Margaret Binnicher.

The Building 8 team was the shipyard softball champion in 1946. On the front row, from the left, are: George Frisbe (manager), Paul Winkle, Wilson Ham, Walter Brennaman, Jimmy Overcash, Eggie Burris, Homer Godfrey, and William "Red" Wood. On the back row, from left, are: Francis Tillman, Adam Hamilton, Willie Griffin, Joe Prather, Earl Cox, Billy Reilly, and Jimmy Budds.

U-2513

In the fall of 1946, the yard overhauled the captured German submarine U-2513. The U-boat was the first submarine to be dry-docked at the yard since before the Second World War. The Type XXI submarine also introduced yard workers to many advanced features that they would incorporate into American submarines in the post-war years.

U-2513 was one of two Type XXI U-boats taken over by the United States Navy at the end of the war. These were in many respects the most advanced submarines that had been built up to that time.

The sleek hull of U-2513 was about 250 feet long and more streamlined than previous submarines. She carried six bow torpedo tubes but no stern tubes like other World War II submarines because of her fine hull lines. Submerged, she displaced 1,819 tons. With twenty-three spare torpedos, her reload capacity was exceptionally large. Loading was simplified by mechanical torpedo handling gear, a vast improvement over the rigging and manhandling of torpedos required in previous submarines.

The propulsion system incorporated two new features. One was an improved snorkle device. This Dutch invention had been developed by the Germans toward the end of the war. It was, in essence, an air intake and exhaust unit, covered with a flapper valve to keep out water from waves, that could be raised like the periscope to provide air to run the diesel engines and carry away their exhaust fumes. In addition, U-2513 carried a huge battery, double the normal capacity, that gave her an exceptionally high underwater speed of sixteen knots.

In the last year of World War II, Hitler embarked on a massive building program for the Type XXI U-boats. The hulls of the vessels were prefabricated in eight sections. After the equipment was installed, each section was shipped by barge to one of three assembly yards at Bremen, Danzig or Hamburg. There the hull sections were welded together and the piping, electrical wiring and other systems connected. Fortunately for the Allied cause, only a small number of Type XXI boats had been completed and commissioned by the time Germany surrendered. U-2513, which

In the fall of 1946, the German submarine U-2513 was repaired at the yard. The Type XXI sub was designed for maximum underwater speed. Her snorkel was the first such device seen by yard workers. American submarines didn't have snorkels until well after World War II.

had been assembled by the Blohm and Vose yard at Hamburg, was one of these. After the collapse of Nazi Germany, the U-boat was surrendered to the Allies at Horten, Norway.

The advanced technology of the vessels greatly influenced the design of American, British and Russian submarines in the years after the war. The United States Navy developed the GUPPY program (for Greater Underwater Propulsive Power) to incorporate the advanced features in American submarines. The GUPPY conversions included removing deck guns, enclosing the periscopes, installing snorkles and remodeling hull lines. Also included was a much larger battery capacity that required an extra section to be inserted in the hull. The Russian Navy operated a number of Type XXI boats after the war and incorporated the design features in their *Whiskey* class diesel submarines.

Before coming to the yard for overhaul, the advanced-design German submarine was closely examined by the top Navy brass. Here, Fleet Admiral Chester W. Nimitz, the Chief of Naval Operations, boards the vessel in May of 1946. On his left, grasping the periscope, is Vice Admiral Forrest Sherman, Deputy CNO.

Shortly after her overhaul at the yard, U-2513 cruises off Key West, Florida. President Truman made a deep dive in the vessel in this area.

"When we were just about ready for our first combat patrol, we had to turn the ship (U-1103) over to another crew and were sent to Hamburg as the future crew of U-2513 which was the Type XXI and built in sections all over the country and finally assembled in the shipyard. Due to heavy air-raid attacks, the completion of U-2513 was delayed while the crew was in training. A short while later, I was transferred to my home town of Danzig where we helped train future commanders. A few days prior to the end of the war, the original crew of U-2513 was replaced with a new crew under command of the highly-decorated ace by the name of Topp. Topp didn't get further than Horten, Norway, an assembly place ordered by the British after the unconditional surrender."

Konrad A. Mueller of Greenville, S. C.,
Control Room Petty Officer of U-2513 during the final construction phase.

SST-1 steams slowly in the Cooper River. The 131-foot-long sub-marine carried a crew of eighteen and was armed with one torpedo tube. Unnamed when she first went into service, the little vessel was later named the Mackerel.

A major project for the Paint Shop in October of 1954 was repair to the hull coating on the small training submarine, SST-1. The hull was covered with neoprene rubber as protection against corro-sion and pitting. Such small submarines were used mostly as targets in fleet exercises.

The Picuda cruises in the Cooper River near the shipyard. She was overhauled twice at the yard, in late 1958 and again in 1961.

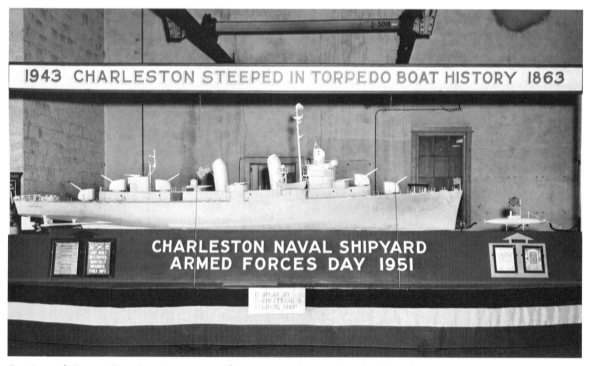

On Armed Forces Day in 1951, many shops set up impressive displays for visitors. Here, a model of a Charleston-built destroyer of World War II dwarfs one of a David torpedo boat of the Civil War era.

Three of the charter members of the Navy Yard Employees Credit Union in 1951. Left to right are Herman Florio of the Planning Division, John B. Florio of Supply who was the credit union's first president, and R. Lockwood Williams of Public Works. Founded in 1936, the Charleston Naval Shipyard Credit Union had 110,000 members by 1985.

C. Allan Ducker receives congratulations from Captain Tillman Dantzler, Shipyard Commander, on his promotion to Master Mechanic, Electronics in November of 1952. In 1968, Ducker became Superintendent of the Electrical-Electronics Group. At the time of his retirement in 1981, he had forty years service at the yard.

Captain Dantzler congratulates Wyman Jean Woods of the Inside Machine Shop on his twenty-dollar award for a beneficial suggestion in December of 1953. Woods was later head of the Outside Machine Shop. At the time of his retirement in 1983, Jean was Superintendent of the Mechanical Group.

Samuel F. Fennessey, Master Mechanic of Public Works, receives a safety trophy from Captain W. M. Johnson, Public Works Officer on 15 June 1956. Shop 07 employees had amassed nearly three million man-hours without a disabling injury. The yard has had the best safety record of any naval shipyard over the years.

These two Liberty Ships arrived in the yard in September of 1954 for conversion to ocean radar vessels, or YAGRs.

The Locator (YAGR-6) became the third Liberty ship the yard had converted to an ocean radar vessel when she was commissioned on 21 January 1956. These vessels were used as part of the nation's air defense early warning system.

In 1951, shipyard supervisiors were being given training on how to decontaminate ships covered with fallout from nuclear weapons. Here James Potter (left) of the Paint Shop applies wet sand over simulated radioactivity while Johnny McDaniel of the Welding Shop stands by to monitor the effectiveness of this technique.

7

Charleston Enters the Nuclear Age

In many ways, the modern era has been the most exciting of any in the shipyard's history.

It has been a time of change, of learning new concepts, of mastering new technologies. The work of the yard has become more technical in nature, requiring more engineering, more detailed planning, and more sophisticated methods of scheduling and control. This has happened because the ships have become incredibly complex, with new propulsion systems, advanced weapons, improved sensors and sophisticated electronics hardware.

THE NEW TECHNOLOGY

To appreciate the changes that have occurred in the yard since the early 1950s, you have to consider the developments in warship design that have taken place since that time. The most revolutionary advance, and one of the first to affect the yard, was nuclear propulsion.

A new era in naval warfare began on 17 January 1955, when *Nautilus*, the first nuclear-powered submarine, embarked on her initial sea trials. Her nuclear reactor produced heat without burning oxygen, making the vessel independent of the atmosphere. For the first time, a submarine was a true submersible, at home in the ocean depths — its endurance limited by the amount of food that could be carried aboard. Every other submarine that had come before was really a surface vessel that could run submerged only for short periods.

Other nuclear-powered submarines quickly followed *Nautilus* to sea. On 21 July 1955 the *Seawolf* was launched and, that same day, the keel was laid for the *Skate* at Electric Boat in Groton, Connecticut. Three more vessels similar to *Skate* had been launched by the summer of 1958, as had the first streamlined hull nuclear-powered submarine, the *Skipjack* (SSN-585). By this time the keels had been laid for ten other nuclear-powered submarines of six different classes. Five shipyards were building the vessels, including the naval yards at Portsmouth, New Hampshire and Mare Island, California — the Navy's prime submarine building yards during World War II.

Her hull showing the ravages of the sea, the Thomas A. Edison (SSBN-610) enters Dry Dock 5 in October of 1966. She was the first ballistic missile submarine to be given a complete overhaul by the yard. This included replacing the fuel in the nuclear reactor.

The first nuclear submarines demonstrated to the world the enormous advantages of nuclear propulsion. In a shakedown cruise from New London to Puerto Rico, *Nautilus* steamed 1,300 miles submerged in eighty-four hours. This was more than ten times further than any other submarine had ever traveled while continuously submerged. It was also the first time a submarine had ever maintained such a high submerged speed — about sixteen knots — for more than an hour. In 1958 *Nautilus* and *Skate* demonstrated the feasibility of winter operations in the Arctic by nuclear submarines. In 1960, the 446-foot-long, two-reactor *Triton* circumnavigated the world, tracing the route of Magellan's historic voyage in eighty-three days, totally independent of the atmosphere.

The driving force behind the nuclear submarine was Admiral Hyman G. Rickover. A tough, forceful man and a brilliant engineer, he created what amounted to a separate navy within the Navy as he ran the Naval Nuclear Propulsion Program with an iron will. Strong measures were essential in the building of the nuclear Navy because a whole new technology had to be created. Many breakthroughs in metallurgy, manufacturing techniques and quality control were required. Rickover attracted talented and loyal people and created with his own staff and those of the two major AEC laboratories associated with the program, Bettis Atomic Power Laboratory near Pittsburgh and Knolls Atomic Power Laboratory in upstate New York, one of the finest engineering organizations ever assembled.

Rickover's standards were high and his methods tough. He recognized the necessity to avoid accidents involving the nuclear reactors and took strong measures to make sure they were built, maintained and operated safely. The people associated with the program were handpicked, thoroughly trained and driven hard. His own personal representatives oversaw all the critical steps in assembling and maintaining the reactors and propulsion plants. He made sure that everyone involved understood that his new program was something special. These same tenets on which Rickover built his program remain in place to this day.

The nuclear-powered attack submarine Skipjack set new submarine speed records when she went into service in 1959. She was the first nuclear submarine to be refueled by the shipyard during an overhaul begun in 1965.

The nuclear submarine imposed completely new requirements on the overhaul shipyards. The new submarines were the most complex and technically sophisticated ships ever built. The reactor cooling system was made of corrosion-resistant metals with which shipyards had little experience machining and welding. Rigorous controls were required to keep the reactor systems surgically clean and prevent foreign matter from getting inside. Once placed in operation, however, the reactor and its primary cooling systems became radioactive as a consequence of the fissioning process that took place in the nuclear fuel. Coping with the radioactivity while doing repairs and making alterations added a new dimension to shipyard work. The most complex work on the reactor was refueling, when the spent nuclear core was removed and replaced with a new one. All the work on the reactor plants was carefully planned and done in "verbatim compliance" with detailed procedures. If the procedure couldn't be followed, the work was stopped, and the procedure evaluated and changed before proceeding. The nature of the work required a discipline on the part of the workers that heretofore had been unknown in a shipyard.

The first major shipyard maintenance work on a nuclear submarine was the initial refueling of the *Nautilus* S2W[1] reactor at Electric Boat in early 1957. Rickover had decided that it was best for the building yards

In September of 1967, the Thomas A. Edison *(SSBN-610) leaves Dry Dock 5.*

---

[1] Naval reactor types are designated by a code. In S2W, "S" stands for the ship type — submarine, "2" for the second reactor design by Westinghouse, "W", the reactor plant contractor. S1W was the *Nautilus* prototype reactor built at the National Reactor Testing Station (now the Idaho National Engineering Laboratory) near Arco, Idaho. The *Skate* used an S3W reactor. *Skipjack* had the first S5W reactor, which became the standard design for nuclear submarines for many years. General Electric also designed naval reactors, such as the S4G type used on the *Triton*. All the Navy's nuclear reactors, with two exceptions, have been of the pressurized water type. The exceptions were the S2G *Seawolf* reactor and its S1G prototype, both used in the 1950s. These were cooled with liquid sodium which proved inappropriate for naval use.

to perform the first refueling of each type reactor. As a consequence, Charleston was one of the later naval shipyards to get involved with this work. Portsmouth became the first naval yard to refuel a nuclear reactor when it accomplished the second refueling of the *Nautilus* in 1959. By this time, *Nautilus* had steamed 153,000 miles on her first two core loads.

The second technological breakthrough in naval warfare that occurred during the 1950s was the development of guided missiles for use aboard ships. The most important of these was the submarine-launched ballistic missile named Polaris for the North Star.

In 1955, President Eisenhower approved the recommendation of the National Security Council to develop a ballistic missile system with a 1,500-mile range. Rear Admiral William F. Raborn was put in charge of the Navy's program to develop such a missile for launching at sea. By the end of 1956, his Special Projects Office of the Bureau of Ordinance was hard at work on a solid fuel, submarine-launched missile they called Polaris. In the summer of 1957, the characteristics of the new Polaris submarine to be built to carry the missiles were approved by the Navy, and the Polaris submarine project was given top priority.

The project gained an even greater sense of urgency that fall. In late August of 1957, the Soviet Union announced that it had succeeded in launching an intercontinental ballistic missile. Scarcely two months later, two Russian *Sputnik* space satellites were circling the earth.

Spurred by the heightened tensions in the Cold War caused by these events, development of the Polaris missile system proceeded at a quickened pace. By early 1958, Electric Boat was building the *George Washington* (SSBN-598), the first submarine which was capable of carrying the missiles. Two years later, on 20 July 1960, *George Washington* launched the first ballistic missiles ever fired by a submerged submarine.[1] On 15 November 1960, she left Charleston on her first deployment, a patrol which lasted sixty-six days, during which she was submerged the entire time.

---

[1] That is, in the post-World War II era. In 1942, the Germans successfully launched small rockets from a submerged U-boat in a test near the island of Peenemünde.

In July of 1960, the George Washington *(SSBN-598) launches her first Polaris A-1 missile. The event marked the beginning of a new era in naval warfare.*

The first Polaris missiles, designated A-1, were twenty-eight feet long, 4½ feet in diameter and weighed about 30,000 pounds. They were two-stage rockets which could deliver a nuclear warhead 1,375 miles. Two improved versions, the A-2 and A-3 models, were later developed. These had longer range, and in the case of the A-3, capability for multiple warheads. Each model of the Polaris missile contained an inertial guidance system which could be programmed for a selected target. In 1985, the Polaris A-3 missiles were still in use in the four ballistic missile submarines of Great Britain.

Along with the Polaris missiles came sophisticated electronics hardware, computers and new navigation equipment for submarines. The accuracy of the missiles depended upon the submarine commander's accurately knowing his ship's position with respect to the earth's surface. The Ships Inertial Navigation System, or SINS, was developed and installed in the George Washington and other ballistic missile submarines for this purpose. Later models worked in conjunction with navigational satellite receivers for increased accuracy. The Polaris missile fire control systems utilized some thirty different computers. These and other electronic components were made in modular form so they could readily be removed for repair and maintenance.

Other missiles followed Polaris in the Navy's submarines. Between 1970 and 1978, the thirty-one newest ballistic missile submarines were fitted for the Poseidon missile. Each Poseidon missile is thirty-four feet long and six feet in diameter and weighs 65,000 pounds. The Poseidon carries multiple, independently-targeted nuclear warheads and has a range of approximately 2,880 miles, similar to the Polaris A-3 missile. In 1979, the longer-range Trident C-4 missile was placed into service. These were fitted in the twelve newest of the Lafayette class ballistic missile submarines, as well as the huge new Ohio class Trident submarines. Missiles launched from torpedo tubes were also developed for nuclear attack submarines. The first of these, the SUBROC anti-submarine missile, was introduced in 1965. In the past few years, the Harpoon anti-ship missile has been added to the attack submarine's arsenal, along with the long-range Tomahawk cruise missile.

While Admiral Raborn was leading the development of the Polaris missile system, work was also proceeding on guided missiles for surface ships. The first of these were the "Three T" missiles: Tartar, Terrier, and Talos. These were surface-to-air missiles, designed to destroy enemy aircraft. Tartar, the smallest of the three, was introduced in the fleet in 1960. The longer-range Terrier and Talos missiles went into service shortly afterwards. These latter two were each a formidable weapon which could carry a nuclear warhead and had a limited capability for use against surface ships and targets on shore. Another missile developed for anti-submarine warfare was the ASROC. This short-range ballistic missile, which has the capability of delivering a nuclear depth bomb, was introduced in 1961. In the 1970s, improved surface-to-air missiles, such as the Standard — MR and the Standard — ER, were placed in service in the fleet.

Improved radar for various applications has been introduced since the mid-1950s. In addition to tracking ships, aircraft and missiles, radar is used to guide surface-to-air and anti-ship missiles.

Many developments have taken place also in anti-submarine warfare, such as the introduction of improved sonar gear. Sonar uses sound to locate objects under water and determine their range. By 1960, nuclear attack submarines were being built with their torpedo tubes positioned amidships to make room for a huge spherical sonar array in the bow. Surface warships were built with a big bulge in their lower bow to house a large sonar array. Eventually, both surface ships and submarines were equipped with towed sonar pods that could be trailed behind the vessels for greater effectiveness.

In 1964, the nuclear-powered warship Bainbridge *was in Dry Dock 5 for repairs. Forward of the superstructure can be seen her eight-cell ASROC launcher and her twin Mark 10 launcher for terrier surface-to-air missiles. She is now designated as a guided missile cruiser, CGN-25.*

THE YARD ENTERS THE NUCLEAR AGE

In early 1956, Rear Admiral Albert G. Mumma, Chief of the Bureau of Ships, announced that Charleston would become a nuclear shipyard. A course in nuclear physics for twenty-four engineers of the Design Division had been started at the yard the previous September. By the summer of 1956 eleven shipyard engineers were taking after-hours courses at the Citadel to learn about nuclear engineering.

Little progress was made in the yard's preparations for nuclear work over the next several years. Admiral Rickover got the Portsmouth and Mare Island shipyards into the business of overhauling nuclear submarines first because these yards had experience building the vessels.

Charleston's first real step in the nuclear propulsion arena came with the conversion of the submarine tender *Proteus*. The shipyard modified the big tender to enable her to support the *George Washington* and other fleet ballistic missile submarines. This work started in January of 1959 and was completed a year-and-a-half later.

In 1959 as work proceeded on the *Proteus*, the Nuclear Power Division was set up in the Planning Department. The new division slowly grew in size over the next few years. The yard's preparations for its first overhaul of a nuclear submarine reactor plant were guided by Commander (later Captain) William S. Humphrey, Jr., who served as Nuclear Power Superintendent for two and one-half years.

In the fall of 1960, the *George Washington* arrived in Charleston to prepare for her first patrol. She and the *Patrick Henry* (SSBN-599), our second ballistic missile submarine, were dry-docked at the yard that year for routine inspections.

It was 1963 when the shipyard began its first nuclear submarine overhaul. The vessel was the *Scorpion*, which was lost at sea in 1968. An overhaul of her sister ship, the *Shark* (SSN-591), followed. In 1965, the *Skipjack*, the world's first streamlined-hull nuclear attack submarine, entered the yard for a complete overhaul, including refueling of her nuclear reactor. Charleston became the first naval yard to refuel an S5W reactor, although the year before Electric Boat had replaced the fuel in a similar reactor on the *George Washington*.

"At that time (1957) we did some modest studies to determine what would be necessary to enable the shipyard to handle nuclear submarines. The studies had to be modest as the one direct approach we made to Admiral Rickover brought back a reply the gist of which was that when he wanted Charleston to handle nuclear submarines he would let us know and not to bother him further."

Captain William Izard Bull, USN, Shipyard Commander 1957-1959

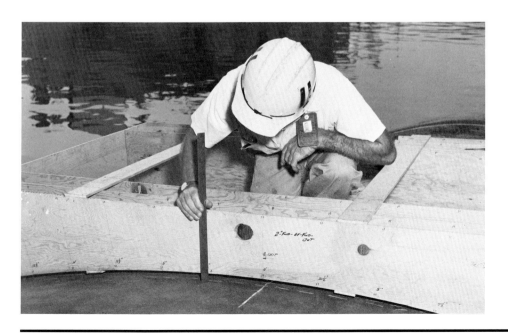

A shipfitter measures the hull of Scorpion (SSN-589) in preparation for building a cofferdam to fit around an opening to be cut in the hull for access to equipment in the vessel. Scorpion was the first nuclear-powered submarine overhauled by the yard.

In July of 1967, the Harder (SS-568) leaves the floating dry dock. She was in the latter stages of a complex overhaul that lasted twenty-five months — the longest ever performed at the yard up to that time.

"Harder, Darter, Trigger, and Trout. They're always in, they never go out."

Popular refrain on the waterfront in the 1960s.

OTHER WORK

As the yard got its feet wet in the nuclear business, a good deal of other overhaul work was accomplished as well. Much was routine overhaul of conventionally-powered submarines and surface ships, but some involved the new, advanced hardware being installed on the Navy's warships.

In 1960, for example, forty-eight ship availabilities were completed by the yard. These included eleven regular overhauls of diesel-powered submarines, two of which belonged to the Turkish government. Fourteen destroyers entered the yard for varied work along with several types of auxiliary vessels.

In the 1960s, the yard updated many destroyers and conventional submarines as part of the Navy's Fleet Modernization Program, or FRAM, for short. In 1961, Charleston gained its first experience with the ASROC system when the missile launchers and associated equipment were installed on three destroyers as part of their FRAM conversions. The FRAM conversion on a destroyer involved considerable work in addition to ASROC installation including rebuilding the ship's superstructure with aluminum. Updated electronics gear was installed, the gun armament reduced, and Mark 32 anti-submarine torpedo tubes fitted.

Another project undertaken by the yard in 1961 was setting up a repair facility for electronic modules from the fire control system of Polaris submarines. This facility was first established in the Electric Shop. Eventually, it became a separate shop known as the Module Maintenance Facility, which was headed by John P. Moore. This is still the Navy's only repair facility for such components used in ballistic missile systems. Similar electronic modules from the four ballistic missile submarines of Great Britain were sent here for repair also. Later, the British Navy set up a similar facility in Scotland and the yard trained many of their technicians.

To enable the yard to better cope with the more sophisticated weapons systems and electronics hardware, the Combat Systems Division was set up in the Planning Department in 1963. During that year, the yard overhauled its first guided missile warship, the *Farragut* (DLG-6). In the years that followed, surface combatant overhauls became increasingly complex and took longer to complete. The yard developed extensive capability to repair and recondition the missile fire control systems, sonars, radars, missile launchers and new communications gear on the warships.

RIVERS DELIVERS

In 1962, work was begun on Dry Dock 5, the biggest construction project at the yard since World War II. The ground-breaking ceremony was held on 16 March. Mendel Rivers had worked hard in Congress for several years to make sure that the $15,600,000 project was funded and carried out as planned. The dry dock was built for the overhaul and maintenance of Polaris submarines, other nuclear-powered ships and surface warships with large bow sonar domes. The new dock was completed and went into service in 1964.

The late 50s and early 60s saw a tremendous expansion of Navy facilities in Charleston that did much to solidify the position of the yard as a shipyard vital to the Navy. In the summer of 1959, a total of thirty-one additional ships were homeported in Charleston. These included Destroyer Squadrons Four and Six and Submarine Squadron Four. In 1960, the Navy's first missile assembly complex was completed at the

Wielding chrome-plated shovels, Representatives Harry R. Sheppard of California (left), and Mendel Rivers break ground for Dry Dock 5 on 16 March 1962. The yard included the $15.6 million project in its 1959 military construction program. Rivers made sure that it was approved and funded.

Naval Ammunition Depot up the river from the yard. Not long afterwards, a fleet ballistic missile training center was built at the Naval Station south of the yard. In 1964, the Charleston Naval Supply Center, which eventually became the Navy's third largest, was created from the Shipyard Supply Department. Additional ships continued to be assigned to the Naval Base. Much of this expansion was the result of the efforts of Congressman Mendel Rivers. Representative Robert Sikes of Florida, a member of the House Appropriations Committee, was credited with saying, "If Rivers puts anything else in Charleston, the whole place will completely sink from sight from the sheer weight of the military installations."

Rivers also kept his eye on the workload of the yard. In late 1964, cutbacks were planned at Charleston and the other naval yards as an economy measure by Secretary of Defense Robert McNamara. Rivers worked with the Navy to have the seaplane tender *Albemarle*, a former escort carrier, sent to Charleston for conversion to a floating aircraft maintenance facility for use by the Army. In 1965, 800 workers per day were employed in conversion of the big vessel which was renamed the *Corpus Christi Bay* (T-ARVH-1).

In the late 1960s, the work of the yard continued to be split between nuclear submarines, diesel submarines and surface vessels. The overhauls of diesel submarines became more difficult because many of the vessels were more than twenty years old and had seen hard service. In 1967, the *Harder* (SS-568) overhaul was finally completed after twenty-five months. This trend was reversed in 1969 and 1970 when the *Bang* (SS-385) overhaul was completed eight days early and at a considerable cost savings. The number of diesel-electric submarines in the fleet was dwindling, however, and in a few years the yard would no longer work on these vessels.

The conversion of the USNS Corpus Christi Bay was completed by the yard in January of 1966. The former World War II escort carrier Albemarle was turned into a floating aircraft maintenance facility for the Army.

In 1970, the yard completed its third major overhaul of a ballistic missile submarine with the *Henry Clay* (SSBN-625) and began a similar overhaul of the *George Washington* (SSBN-598). During this period, the Navy moved to strengthen the organizations of the naval shipyards to better cope with the new technologies. In 1969, the shipyard Radiological Control Office had been formed under J. H. Riley. In January of 1970, E. A. (Red) Rice became the first civilian Nuclear Power Superintendent at the yard and the next year the Nuclear Power Division became a separate department with Rice as Nuclear Engineering Manager. During this period, nuclear managers reporting directly to the Shipyard Commander were established in the Quality Assurance, Planning, and Production Departments. In 1971, the Combat Systems Office was set up under T. M. McManus to provide more technical control over work related to missile fire control systems, sonar, radar, and related electronics hardware.

From The Worst To the Best

Despite the strengthened shipyard technical organizations, the yard experienced considerable difficulty with overhaul and repair work in the early 1970s. Between November of 1971 and November of 1972, the yard started major refueling overhauls of three nuclear submarines, the heaviest workload on these complex vessels that had been undertaken up to that point. The work on each of the three submarines fell behind schedule. A Navy study indicated that worker productivity was low at the yard. Admiral Rickover in April of 1973 called the shipyard "the worst in the nation." The Shipyard Commander, Captain John Woolston, said that he could not disagree. Senator Ernest Hollings joined the fray, blaming the problems at the yard on poor management.

E. A. (Red) Rice joined the Nuclear Power Division in May of 1960, after serving for three years as a navigator in the U. S. Air Force following his graduation from Clemson University. In 1969, Rice was named the first civilian Nuclear Power Superintendent at the yard. The next year Red became Nuclear Engineering Manager, as Nuclear Engineering became a separate department. Over the years, Rice has had a greater influence than any other individual in shaping the course of nuclear propulsion plant work at the yard.

The nuclear-powered attack submarine Ray (SSN-653) at sea in December of 1976, shortly after being overhauled at the yard. The yard completed the complex overhaul of the Sturgeon class vessel three and one-half months ahead of schedule. This outstanding achievement heralded a breakthrough in improved performance of nuclear submarine work by the yard.

In February of 1983, the yard began its first overhaul of a conventional submarine in many years when the Bonefish (SS-582) arrived. The work was completed thirteen and one-half months later.

To alleviate this situation, a decision was made on a course of action that would serve to reduce workload backlog, the major cause of the problem. In order to maintain high standards of workmanship while not sacrificing the integrity of the shipyard, a decision was made to concentrate the shipyard's overhaul efforts by essentially performing work on one ship at a time. Over a period of time, the three submarine overhauls were completed. A hiatus in nuclear work followed, during which time the yard developed improved methods of scheduling and controlling work on nuclear submarines. These new methods paid off when the Ray (SSN-653) overhaul was completed in 1976, three and one-half months ahead of schedule. Since that time, Charleston has been a leader among shipyards, both naval and private, in completing nuclear-powered submarine overhauls on, or ahead of, schedule.

In the 1970s, the yard continued overhauling surface warships and auxiliary vessels. In 1978, completion of a complex overhaul of the cruiser Richmond K. Turner (CG-20) marked the twenty-fifth overhaul of a guided missile warship by the yard. The work on Turner included installation of the Harpoon anti-ship missile system.

Also, in the late 1970s, a new Navy policy in overhaul of warships evolved. Longer periods were scheduled between major overhauls. Shorter limited availabilities, many performed at remote refit sites, were accomplished in between the extended overhauls. As a result, the yard has performed more work at remote sites in the last few years.

In early 1984, Charleston was named the best naval shipyard in the nation when Captain Richard G. Camacho, the Shipyard Commander, accepted the Chief of Naval Material Productivity Excellence Award. A main reason was the yard's outstanding performance in overhauling the ballistic missile submarine Mariano G. Vallejo (SSBN-658) in record time.

This award signified a remarkable comeback in performance of work at the yard, from "the worst in the nation" in 1973 to the best in the business a decade later.

On 25 April 1984, Vice Admiral Earl B. Fowler, Commander of Naval Sea Systems Command, presents the Chief of Naval Material Productivity Excellence Award to Captain Richard G. Camacho, the Shipyard Commander. This award recognized Charleston as the best naval shipyard in the business. Six months later, the yard also received the Chief of Naval Material Management Effectiveness Award.

The Yard's first radiation monitors class, circa 1960, is given a demonstration of the proper method for calibrating a radiation detection instrument. Wilfred S. Kearse, third from right, was one of the key people in the yard's health physics program in the early years. A quarter-century after this photograph was taken, he was still a supervisor in the Radiological Control Office.

J. H. (Jack) Riley came to work at the yard in 1965 as an engineer in the Nuclear Power Division. A Kentucky native and a graduate of the Merchant Marine Academy, Riley became the first shipyard Director of Radiological Control in 1970, a position he still held fifteen years later.

J. B. Lackey, an electrician who became head of the Temporary Service Shop and later Nuclear Production Manager, helped lead the yard to dramatic improvements in nuclear propulsion plant work in the late 1970s. Lackey served at the yard for nearly forty years.

Conversion Of The Proteus

A submarine tender is a mother ship whose task it is to keep her brood ready for sea. The tender is a small floating shipyard, one that can repair anything from a valve or pump to a faulty torpedo. The tender also furnishes her submarines with equipment ranging from spare electronics hardware to the latest movies.

As work proceeded on the Polaris missile program and construction of the first missile-firing submarine, the *George Washington*, it was recognized that this special submarine would require a special submarine tender. The tender would be the *Proteus*. The job of Charleston Naval Shipyard would be to convert the big tender, which had been been built during World War II, to provide the necessary support facilities for not only the nuclear reactor plant of the *George Washington*, but also the huge Polaris missiles she was capable of carrying as well.

The *Proteus* arrived at the yard on 15 January 1959. To provide room for the extra equipment, it was decided to cut the ship apart and add a new forty-four-foot-long plug amidships. The shipyard Design Division developed plans to construct the new plug in twelve sections. In charge of the project was R. E. Lapin. Other engineers involved with the work included Jack Day, John D. Wilcox and Dan Berry.

Buck Rourk of the Outside Machine Shop and Jack T. Day of the Design Division check the master level plate used to measure list and trim of the aft section of the Proteus as it is floated in the dry dock. Day was a key figure in the Nuclear Power Division in the early years of nuclear propulsion plant work at the yard. In 1976, he became Director of Management Engineering.

In early 1959, the Proteus (AS-19) rests at a pier as the yard makes preparations to move her into dry dock for conversion to the first fleet ballistic missile submarine tender.

The *Proteus* was placed in Dry Dock 1, the huge vessel nearly filling the dock. On 8 and 9 June of 1959, the hull was sliced through, cutting the ship in half. The aft end of the vessel was sealed and the dock flooded. The aft section was then carefully floated into position to provide room for the forty-four-foot plug.

The new section of the ship was put in place piece-by-piece. It contained seventy separate spaces that the yard had to fit out. Some 320 other spaces aboard the vessel were rearranged to some degree. New equipment, including a huge crane, was installed to handle Polaris missiles. A magazine designed to hold twenty spare missiles was built into the ship. Special facilities were installed to support work related to nuclear submarine reactor plants. Radiation shielding, designed under subcontract by Electric Boat, was put in place. The electric-generating capacity of the ship was increased to 15,000 kilowatts, enough power to run the entire shipyard. The project cost some $26,000,000 and was the biggest conversion job done by the yard since the Second World War.

One of the more challenging engineering problems encountered had to do with thermal expansion and resulting stresses in the hull as the new hull section was being welded. The new section was made of HY80, the high-strength steel used for the pressure hull of modern submarines. This was the yard's first experience with HY80, which expanded with temperature changes at a different rate from the rest of the hull. The thermal expansion and contraction problems were resolved by keeping the ship as near a constant temperature as practical. This was done by use of a special sprinkler system that sprayed water to cool the hull during the day, and by painting the decks of the ship white to reduce the temperature rise in the hot sun. The welding was done at night during the cooler hours.

In June of 1960, the work was completed. The *Proteus* left for sea trials on 6 July 1960. The trials were a complete success except for a three-hour delay at sea when the ship's rudder failed to return to position because a small rubber gasket failed. With completion of the *Proteus* conversion, the yard had taken its first step into the nuclear age.

On 8 June 1959, the stern section of the Proteus is floated into position, forty-four feet aft, to provide room for the new center section. It took two days to slice through the big ship's hull.

Here the aft section of the ship is ready to accept the forty-four-foot plug. The forward part of the vessel was partially flooded when the aft section was repositioned, so that the forward end would remain firmly in place.

The plug was constructed in place. Twelve major sub-assemblies were prefabricated, the heaviest of which weighed some forty-seven tons. In this view, a wing tank section is being installed.

Shipyard welders make the final welds on the underside of the hull. This was the yard's first experience with welding HY 80 high-strength steel used in the pressure hull of modern American submarines.

A Polaris missile canister is lowered into place in the missile magazine on the main deck level. Much of the work associated with the conversion related to installation of special missile-handling facilities.

The conversion of Proteus was completed on 8 July 1960. Note the huge missile-handling crane support structure amidships.

USS GEORGE WASHINGTON

"In any operation, and under all circumstances, a decisive naval superiority is to be considered as a fundamental principle."

GEORGE WASHINGTON

Our first President believed in a strong Navy, but he could hardly have imagined his namesake.

No ship in history had ever carried such awesome firepower as the *George Washington* (SSBN-598), America's first nuclear-powered ballistic missile submarine. She combined the speed and endurance of nuclear propulsion with long-range missiles that could be fired while she was hidden under the sea.

She had been built at Electric Boat in Groton, Connecticut, actually starting out as a nuclear attack submarine. The partially completed hull of *Scorpion* (SSN-589) was cut in two and a 130-foot-long section inserted to house the sixteen Polaris missiles. Renamed *George Washington*, she was launched in June of 1959.

By 1968, forty of her sister ships were also at sea. The first four were like her, the others even bigger and designed from scratch to carry the huge ballistic missiles. The fleet of forty-one was built to keep the peace. Unlike warships that came before, their success lay in never being called upon in combat. They hid underneath the sea in the vast oceans, undetected but nonetheless a constant reminder to an enemy that an attack on America would bring devastating retaliation.

So important were they to our country's defense, they were manned by two different crews to keep the vessels at sea as much as possible. One was called the Blue Crew and the other the Gold Crew; after each fifty-six-day patrol they would change.

The *George Washington* was a frequent visitor to the yard. In 1960, she became the first ballistic missile submarine to be dry-docked here. Two years later she was in dry dock at the yard again for minor work. In 1970, she was given her second complete overhaul, and her nuclear reactor was refueled by the yard.

On 24 January 1985, the *George Washington* was retired from the fleet when she was decommissioned at Puget Sound Naval Shipyard. In the words of Lieutenant G. D. Gibson, in his invocation at the ceremony, she was "the ultimate memorial to peace - the unused weapon." The missile compartment of the submarine was removed to comply with arms limitation agreements prior to the decommissioning, returning the vessel to the same configuration as when she had started out twenty-seven years before.

In June of 1962, the George Washington enters dry dock at the yard for minor repairs.

In April of 1969, her overhaul nearly completed, the James Monroe (SSBN-622) undergoes final testing at a yard pier.

Standing tall, the piper, a crew member of HMS Resolution, personifies Great Britain's pride in her first ballistic missile submarine. The vessel received a shakedown availability at the yard in January of 1968 before loading Polaris missiles for test firing in the Atlantic Range.

FRAM conversions to modernize diesel-powered submarines often included lengthening the hull to provide room for additional machinery. Here in early 1961 the stern portion of the hull of Trumpetfish (SS-425) is in position ready to receive the new plug.

A portion of the new hull section is formed in the Shipfitters Shop.

The new hull section is moved to the vessel by truck.

Workmen watch from the side of the dry dock as the new hull plug is lowered into place.

The operator of Portal Crane 31 completes installation of the plug, which lengthens the submarine by some eighteen feet.

In the fall of 1961, preservationists throughout the Southeast were concerned with the fate of the Marshlands Plantation house. It had to be moved to make room for the new dry dock. Although the Navy offered to donate the historic house to the city, there was no money available, at first, to move it to a suitable location.

On 28 August 1961, Charleston mayor J. Palmer Gaillard, Jr. announced that arrangements had been made with the College of Charleston to move Marshlands to Fort Johnson. Here, resting on two barges, the house is moved through Charleston Harbor.

Tugs nudge the house to its new site at Fort Johnson, a journey of nine miles from the shipyard. Today the historic house, its ante-bellum splendor restored, commands a magnificent view of Charleston Harbor.

A Dry Dock From Mendel Rivers

In early 1962, dredging of the cavity for the huge graving dock was well underway.

By November of 1962, the evacuation for the dry dock was nearing completion. The wooden cofferdams at the head of the dry dock were filled with earth.

In April of 1964, the Andrew Jackson (SSBN-619) became the first vessel to enter Dry Dock 5. She was in the yard for a three month post-shakedown availability.

In November of 1966, Rear Admiral Batcheller shows the yard's new dry dock to U. S. Senator Ernest Hollings. Senator Hollings has been a frequent visitor to the yard over the years.

In 1949, the yard chapter of the Naval Civilian Administrators Association was founded to promote the interests of the yard. These men were the NCAA members, circa 1963. Left to right, front row: H. Nathan, Code 260; W. Prentiss, Code 630; T. McManus, Code 190; C. McNeil, Code 250; J. Melton, Code 302; R. Lapin, Code 250/131; R. Bailey, Code 138. Second row: E. Smith, Code 230; M. Gabis, Code 730; J. Thomas, Code 700; H. Wotring, Code 134; V. Johnston, Code 225; J. Sollar, Jr., Code 860; N. Edwards, Code 110.
Third row: H. Chilcott, Code 385; J. Andersen, Code 402; W. Schachte, Code 242; W. Lown, Code 620; E. Figg, Code 150; J. Smith, Code 170; R. Willeford, Code 113.
Fourth row: K. Long, Code 385; H. Hoppman, Code 375/930; W. Limehouse, Code 440; C. Warner, Code 2300.

The Shark (SSN-591) was the second nuclear-powered submarine overhauled by the yard. Here she is in Dry Dock 5 beside the guided missile cruiser Bainbridge in the fall of 1964.

In 1970, the overhaul of the Bang (SS-385) was completed eight days ahead of schedule. This was a breakthrough for the yard which had been taking much longer than planned to complete diesel submarine overhauls for several years.

John J. Dodds, Master Electrician, is presented a safety achievement flag in 1966 by Rear Admiral Edgar H. Batcheller, Shipyard Commander. After his retirement in 1974 Dodds served with distinction as mayor of Mt. Pleasant.

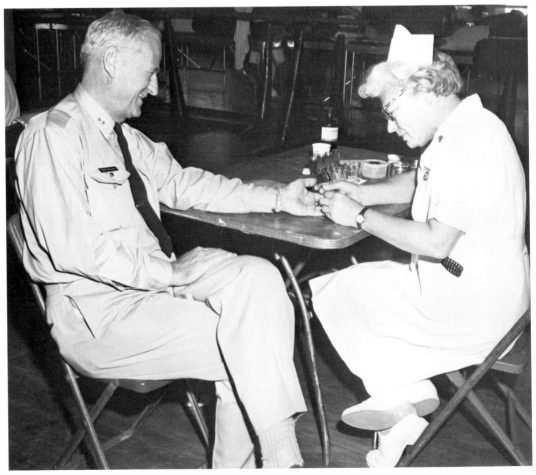

Rear Admiral Batcheller sets an example for his employees by donating blood in November of 1966. Yard workers remember him as an impressive figure during his visits to the waterfront, always with his swagger stick in hand.

In 1969, Ronald T. Redick (left) and Frank Winchester of the Electric Shop prepare electrical leads on the main propulsion generator from the Trigger (SS-564).

In October of 1965, Margaret Miller of the Inside Machine Shop manufactures threaded fasteners on her turret lathe. In the 1960s and 1970s, more women began to be employed in non-traditional jobs at the yard.

Shipyard divers Frank Ash (in water) and Chuck Richards (center), and rigger Jimmy Dehay (right) remove the propeller from the Dewey (DDG-45) in August of 1984. Over the years the shipyard diving team has made many innovations in underwater work on naval ships.

Water pours into Dry Dock 2 as U. S. Congressman Mendel Rivers smiles for the photographer. With Congressman Rivers in this 1968 photograph is Rear Admiral Herman Kossler, the Naval Base Commander. This was one of Rivers' last visits to "his navy yard."

In November of 1975, U. S. Senator Strom Thurmond is shown an example of work done by the shipyard machinists by C. S. Stimson, Mechanical Group Superintendent.

In December of 1972, Reverend Bob Harrington, the renowned "Chaplain of Bourbon Street," visited the yard. He gave a stirring "God and country" speech intended to motivate yard workers to better performance.

Welder Frank Huff, here at his retirement in 1984, was a splendid example of a skilled shipyard tradesman. Many considered him one of the finest welders ever to work at the yard. He also served as a welding training instructor for many years. Standing behind Huff is T. W. Grady, Structural Group Superintendent.

Over the years, working at the yard has often been a family affair. One of the best-known shipyard families is the Cercopelys. Shown here are representatives from three generations. From the left in this 1977 photograph are Clarence Cercopely, Don Mauchline, Dee Cercopely, Gene Cercopely, and Ellen Cercopely Mauchline. Clarence started it all when he came to work in the Boiler Shop in 1913. Gene, one of Clarence's four sons who worked at the yard, began in 1935 as a welder. Dee and Ellen are Clarence's grandchildren, and are only two of many third-generation Cercopelys working at the yard.

The Luce (DDG-7) entered the yard in August of 1967 for over-haul. She was the first warship on which the yard installed the FAST (Fast Automatic Shuttle Transfer) missile-handling system.

In 1974, the Wainwright (CG-28) was in the yard for a complex overhaul. About two-thirds of the yard's workload in 1974 was on surface ships.

In April of 1968, yard workers lower a five-inch gun mount in place on a destroyer.

In 1978, the Richmond K. Turner (CG-20) became the twenty-fifth guided missile ship to be overhauled by the yard and the first to have the Harpoon anti-ship missile system installed. The Turner is a "double-ender," with missile launchers both forward and aft. Both of her Mark 10 launchers were overhauled and modernized by the yard.

A test of the main ballast tank emergency blow system is conducted on the Darter (SS-576) in January of 1967. Behind the Darter is the Atule (SS-403).

Two World War II vintage destroyers were in dry dock together undergoing overhaul in July of 1969. The yard overhauled ten destroyers that year.

One of the most complex submarine over-hauls undertaken by the yard was that of Narwhal (SSN-671), completed in January of 1982. The shipyard began detailed planning for the work more than two years before the start of the overhaul.

In June of 1982, a 310-ton portal crane is lowered in place on the floating dry dock Oak Ridge (ARDM-1) at Kings Bay, Georgia. This was the heaviest crane lift ever made by the yard.

In January of 1983, the CNS Battery Tiger Team completed its one hundredth battery renewal on the attack submarine Sturgeon at the Charleston Naval Station. Over the past two decades, the shipyard Tiger Teams have earned a well-deserved reputation for outstanding service to the fleet at remote sites.

Left to right, First Row: R. W. Nusbaum, E. A. Biering, A. R. Bischoff, J. R. Dehay, C. E. Seabrook, J. J. Smith, I. Jackson, F. Roach (Gould Rep.).

Second Row: J. E. Cooper, D. E. Briggs, A. Macklin, V. C. Roach, B. G. Bollard, H. B. Hodge, C. A. Thomas, J. A. Garret, E. Anderson (NAVSEA 56ZF).

Third Row: E. Guingona, J. Smith, A. Solomon, C. Colello, E. F. Strickland, M. W. Howard, F. E. Taylor, R. May, C. A. Mincey, B. E. Chandler, C. M. Shingler, J. W. Stocks, R. Chambers (NAVSEA 56ZF).

Fourth Row: M. R. Harper, W. E. Crump, S. J. Richter, W. D. Black, T. M. Crosby, W. F. Ferrette, M. W. Macchio, J. L. Dennis, D. L. Dennis, W. C. Roberts, N. C. Haga, P. W. Olliff.

Not Present: D. M. Alston, J. M. Reubish, H. A. Nobles.

Palmer W. Olliff displays an exhibit set up for the Shipyard Museum. Olliff, who came to the yard in 1941 as an apprentice sheet-metal worker, has long been the unofficial shipyard historian.

The Shipyard Museum is located on the aircraft carrier Yorktown at the Patriots Point Naval and Maritime Museum. Palmer Olliff was the driving force behind establishment of the Shipyard Museum in 1981.

This display was prepared by the yard Rigger Shop. Many yard workers contributed their time and effort to help set up the museum.

Palmer W. Olliff photograph.

In September of 1978 when difficulty was encountered in plans to put an E-1B radar plane on the Yorktown, the yard came to the rescue. Here the floating crane YD-235, which normally alternates between the yard and the Naval Weapons Station, gently lifts the aircraft aboard the big carrier.

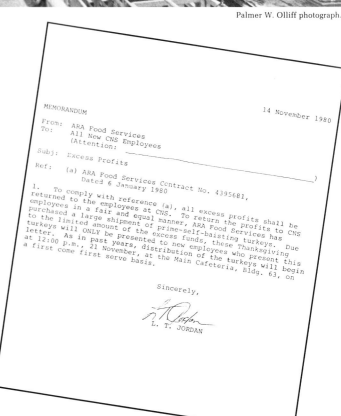

MEMORANDUM   14 November 1980

From: ARA Food Services
To: All New CNS Employees
         (Attention: _____)

Subj: Excess Profits

Ref: (a) ARA Food Services Contract No. 4395681,
             Dated 6 January 1980

1.   To comply with reference (a), all excess profits shall be returned to the employees at CNS. To return the profits to CNS employees in a fair and equal manner, ARA Food Services has purchased a large shipment of prime-self-baisting turkeys. Due to the limited amount of the excess funds, these Thanksgiving turkeys will ONLY be presented to new employees who present this letter. As in past years, distribution of the turkeys will begin at 12:00 p.m., 21 November, at the Main Cafeteria, Bldg. 63, on a first come first serve basis.

                                              Sincerely,

                                              L. T. JORDAN

A "turkey letter." Over the years, new yard employees have often been presented such ersatz letters, much to the consternation of food service workers. The tradition dates back to well before World War II.

196

Visitors to the yard still pass by the little park at Memorial Square. The bell came from the cruiser Charleston which was decommissioned in 1923. The four muzzle-loading cannons came from the Lancaster, a steam sloop-of-war built before the Civil War.

In 1982, the yard opened its facilities to families of workers for the first time in many years. Here Raymond W. Roberts, foreman welder, shows off some of the hardware used by the Welding Shop.

Congressional Record

PROCEEDINGS AND DEBATES OF THE 98th CONGRESS, SECOND SESSION

United States of America

No. 48

WASHINGTON, THURSDAY, APRIL 12, 1984

Vol. 130

Senate

CHARLESTON NAVAL SHIPYARD RECEIVES 1983 PRODUCTIVITY

Mr. HOLLINGS. Mr. President, the Charleston, S.C. Naval Shipyard has been selected by the Chief of Naval Material (CNM) to receive the CNM Productivity Excellence Award for fiscal year 1983. This award establishes Charleston as the leading naval shipyard in the United States.

This only confirms what has been evident for a long period of time. When it comes to excellence—and a standard of performance that well exceeds their competition—the workers at Charleston stand alone. The award is a fitting tribute to the skills, reliability, and loyalty of every employee in the yard, from nuclear engineer to pipefitter to laborer. I believe that they all richly deserve this award. In my view, the Charleston team has consistently outperformed any shipyard—be it public or private—in the world.

I call to your attention the many areas of competition where the Charleston workers excelled: Ship overhaul durations, total savings or cost avoidances resulting from productivity improvements, customer satisfaction on the quality of work accomplished, overhauls completed within cost, quality of worklife, quality circles, employee suggestion program, worker motivation seminars, relationships with community, local, and State organizations, and a record contribution of $417,000 to the Combined Federal Campaign.

During fiscal year 1983, Charleston completed all 14 availabilities on time or early, returning over 155 operating days to the fleet. This fantastic record, along with the development of a corporate management plan, and winning the National Safety Council Award for job safety were the most outstanding accomplishments cited in the CNM Award.

The people of Charleston are justifiably proud of all their accomplishments. They are equally proud that they can serve the Navy and their country so well. Excellence is a tradition at Charleston. I am very proud for every worker in the navy yard for the recognition of a job well done. I anticipate that this may become an annual event.

Mr. President, I ask unanimous consent that the Charleston Shipyard's press release on the award be inserted in the RECORD.

There being no objection, the press release was ordered to be printed in the RECORD, as follows:

[News release, Jan. 30, 1984]
CHARLESTON NAVAL SHIPYARD—PRESS RELEASE

Charleston Naval Shipyard, one of South Carolina's largest employers, has been selected to receive the Chief of Naval Material (CNM) Productivity Excellence Award for Fiscal Year 1983. This award establishes Charleston as the leading Naval shipyard in the United States.

In a message to Captain R. G. Camacho, Shipyard Commander, Admiral S. A. White, Chief of Naval Material, stated: "It is my pleasure to personally congratulate you and your command for having been selected as the winner of the 1983 Productivity Excellence Award within your competitive category. The extraordinary efforts invested in improvements to both productivity and quality of work life are reflected in the superior level of performance of your command. The results have been evident in the outstanding, creative, quality-oriented results you have achieved this year. I applaud your accomplishments. Please pass my thanks to all hands. Well done."

Charleston Naval Shipyard competed in the areas of ship overhaul scheduled durations, total savings or cost avoidance resulting from productivity improvements, customer satisfaction on the quality of work accomplished, overhauls completed within cost, quality of work life, Quality Circles, Employee Suggestion Program, worker motivation seminars, relationships with community, local and state organizations, and record contributions to the Combined Federal Campaign. During the last Fiscal Year, Charleston completed all fourteen availabilities on time or early, returning over 155 operating days to the fleet. Cited as outstanding accomplishments were the early ship completions, the development of a Corporate Management Plan, and winning the National Safety Council award for job safety.

Because employee involvement and dedication are recognized by NAVMAT as essential to productivity improvement, the award contains provisions for the special recognition of selected employees who will be recognized as CNM Productivity "Fellows". The fellowship awards are presented to individuals who made a substantial contribution to productivity excellence within the organization. The employees selected will be recognized at an award ceremony and they will be presented a special lapel pin by Admiral White. Additionally, every shipyard employee will be awarded a wallet-sized card citing their contribution.

Commenting on the award, Captain R. G. Camacho stated: "This is the premier award and means that we have been recognized as the number one shipyard by two higher echelons of command. I always believed that our people were the best, and NAVSEA and NAVMAT have confirmed that belief. Our people have worked hard; their efforts have paid off; and now they are being recognized. I am indeed proud to serve as Commander of Charleston Naval Shipyard."

The award, which consists of an engraved plaque and a flag for public display, will be presented next month in Charleston by the Chief of Naval Material, Admiral S. A. White.

The yard completed a major overhaul of the ballistic missile submarine Mariano G. Vallejo (SSBN-658) in July of 1984, finishing 147 days ahead of schedule. This was the first overhaul of a ballistic missile submarine by the yard in ten years, since the dark days of the early 70s.

Drawing by Eugene Davis

In 1982, the yard received the Governor's Large Employer-of-the-Year award for employment of the handicapped. Standing with Shipyard Commander W. J. Mahony with the award are four key figures in the yard program for employing handicapped people. From the left, are David L. Day, supervisory administrative support assistant; Carolyn H. Gorman, personnel assistant; William T. Hutchison, personnel staffing specialist; Captain Mahony and Denver George, toolroom mechanic general foreman.

In June of 1985, Thomas B. Cooper, Director of Industrial Relations, received the prestigious John E. Fogarty Public Personnel Award for his contributions to employment of the handicapped. Cooper, a native South Carolinian and a Citadel graduate, became Director of Industrial Relations in 1980.

John Sneed admires a plaque recognizing the yard as the winner of the Navy's 1984 Environmental Protection Award as Captain Dean H. Hines, Shipyard Commander, looks on. The yard received the award for its outstanding environmental protection programs. Sneed, the 1984 shipyard employee-of-the-year, is head of the Environmental Engineering and Waste Management Branch of the Public Works Department.

Commandants And Commanders Of The Shipyard

Commandants of the Charleston Navy Yard	Assumed Command
Captain Edwin Longnecker	August 1, 1902
Captain R. M. Berry	September 1, 1904
Rear Admiral E. S. Prime	May 15, 1905
Commander S. W. Very	September 1, 1905
Commander J. A. H. Nichols	November 18, 1905
Commodore G. L. Dyer	April 9, 1906
Rear Admiral J. D. Adams	January 2, 1909
Rear Admiral C. E. Fox	June 3, 1909
Rear Admiral J. M. Helm	October 13, 1911
Rear Admiral J. R. Edwards	October 2, 1914
Rear Admiral B. C. Bryan	July 8, 1915
Rear Admiral E. A. Anderson	November 8, 1919
Captain R. E. Pope	May 22, 1922
Rear Admiral A. P. Niblack	July 19, 1922
Rear Admiral G. W. Williams	August 12, 1923
Captain M. E. Trench	September 10, 1924
Captain F. A. Traut	September 5, 1925
Rear Admiral N. A. McCully	September 1, 1927
Captain J. N. Ferguson	June 15, 1931
Rear Admiral J. J. Raby	September 12, 1931
Captain W. A. Hall	January 15, 1934
Rear Admiral E. B. Fenner	May 14, 1934
Captain J. S. Abbott	March 9, 1936
Rear Admiral H. V. Butler	July 17, 1936
Rear Admiral W. H. Allen	March 7, 1938
Rear Admiral W. A. Glassford	June 2, 1942
Rear Admiral Jules James	May 14, 1943
Rear Admiral L. T. DuBose	November 13, 1945

Commanders, Charleston
Naval Shipyard   *Assumed Command*

Commodore R. N. S. Baker .... 30 November 1945
Captain H. C. Sexton .... 28 April 1947
Captain Logan McKee .... 2 May 1949
Rear Admiral Logan McKee .... 1 June 1951
Captain Oscar Stiegler .... 29 September 1951
Captain T. T. Dantzler .... 8 October 1951
Captain H. J. Pfingstag .... 3 August 1954
Captain W. I. Bull .... 27 September 1957
Captain R. B. Madden .... 2 December 1959
Rear Admiral E. A. Wright .... 13 September 1960
Rear Admiral E. H. Batcheller .... 25 April 1963
Captain C. N. Payne, Jr. .... 10 July 1968
Rear Admiral C. N. Payne, Jr. .... 16 September 1969
Captain J. Woolston .... 23 March 1971
Rear Admiral J. B. Berude .... 30 November 1973
Rear Admiral C. S. Davis, Jr. .... 22 May 1975
Captain W. J. Mahony .... 22 July 1978
Captain R. G. Camacho .... 7 August 1982
Captain D. H. Hines .... 13 June 1984

Vessels Built By The Shipyard

Name	Number	Type	Launched
Pee Dee	—	snag boat	1913
Wateree	—	snag boat	1913
—	YSD-1	seaplane wrecking derrick	1916
Brunswick	—	tender	1916
Wando	YT-17	yard tug	03-17-16
Wave	YFB-10	ferry boat	08-31-16
—	SC-106	sub chaser	10-31-17
—	SC-107	sub chaser	11-15-17
—	SC-108	sub chaser	11-15-17
—	SC-109	sub chaser	12-15-17
—	SC-110	sub chaser	02-18-18
—	SC-111	sub chaser	03-02-18
—	SC-112	sub chaser	03-20-18
—	SC-113	sub chaser	04-04-18
Asheville	PG-21	gunboat	07-04-18
—	YT-46	yard tug	04-29-19
—	YT-47	yard tug	04-24-19
—	YC-534	coal barge	1919
—	YE-31	ammunition lighter	05-21-19
Tillman	DD-135	destroyer	07-07-19
—	YC-535	coal barge	11-12-19
Tulsa	PG-22	gunboat	08-25-22
—	YT-55	yard tug	10-08-25
—	YO-40	oil barge	12-10-28
—	YG-13	garbage lighter	08-29-29
—	YG-14	garbage lighter	08-29-29
—	YMT-13	motor tug	05-17-32
Calumet	CG-61	harbor cutter	09-28-34
Navesink	CG-63	harbor cutter	09-28-34
Tuckahoe	CG-64	harbor cutter	09-28-34
Charleston	PG-51	gunboat	02-25-36
Bibb	CG-71	coast cutter	01-14-37
Osceola	YT-129	yard tug	03-03-38
—	YT-132	yard tug	07-18-38
Sterett	DD-407	destroyer	10-27-38
Massasoit	YT-131	yard tug	12-13-38
Roe	DD-418	destroyer	06-21-39
Heekon	YT-141	yard tug	11-29-39
Nokomis	YT-142	yard tug	11-29-39
Jones	DD-427	destroyer	12-14-39
—	YT-143	yard tug	04-22-40
Grayson	DD-435	destroyer	08-07-40
Swanson	DD-443	destroyer	11-02-40
—	YCF-13	car float	06-24-40
—	YSD-10	seaplane wrecking derrick	08-15-40
—	YT-144	yard tug	08-29-40
—	YSD-12	seaplane wrecking derrick	12-12-40
—	YSD-13	seaplane wrecking derrick	12-12-40
Ingraham	DD-444	destroyer	02-15-41
—	YSD-16	seaplane wrecking derrick	04-15-41
—	YSD-21	seaplane wrecking derrick	04-15-41
Corry	DD-463	destroyer	07-28-41
Hobson	DD-464	destroyer	09-08-41
Beatty	DD-640	destroyer	12-20-41
Tillman	DD-641	destroyer	12-20-41
—	YSD-28	seaplane wrecking derrick	03-14-42
Pringle	DD-477	destroyer	05-02-42
Stanly	DD-478	destroyer	05-02-42
Stevens	DD-479	destroyer	06-24-42
Bell	DD-587	destroyer	06-24-42
Burns	DD-588	destroyer	08-08-42
Izard	DD-589	destroyer	08-08-42
—	LST-353	tank landing ship	10-12-42
—	LST-354	tank landing ship	10-13-42

Vessels Built By The Shipyard

Name	Number	Type	Launched
—	LST-355	tank landing ship	11-16-42
—	LST-356	tank landing ship	11-16-42
—	LST-357	tank landing ship	12-14-42
—	LST-358	tank landing ship	12-15-42
—	LST-359	tank landing ship	01-11-43
—	LST-360	tank landing ship	01-11-43
—	YSD-33	seaplane wrecking derrick	02-25-43
—	YSD-34	seaplane wrecking derrick	02-25-43
Hamilton	DD-590	destroyer	04-07-43
Twiggs	DD-591	destroyer	04-07-43
Grant	DD-649	destroyer	05-29-43
Bryant	DD-665	destroyer	05-29-43
Manning	DE-199	destroyer escort	06-01-43
Neuendorf	DE-200	destroyer escort	06-01-43
Craig	DE-201	destroyer escort	07-22-43
Eichenberger	DE-202	destroyer escort	07-22-43
—	YSD-59	seaplane wrecking derrick	07-31-43
Newman	DE-205	destroyer escort	08-09-43
Liddle	DE-206	destroyer escort	08-09-43
Thomason	DE-203	destroyer escort	08-23-43
Jordan	DE-204	destroyer escort	08-23-43
Kephart	DE-207	destroyer escort	09-06-43
Cofer	DE-208	destroyer escort	09-06-43
Lloyd	DE-209	destroyer escort	10-23-43
Otter	DE-210	destroyer escort	10-23-43
Hubbard	DE-211	destroyer escort	11-11-43
Hayter	DE-212	destroyer escort	11-11-43
Powell	DE-213	destroyer escort	11-27-43
Chaffe	DE-230	destroyer escort	11-27-43
Hodges	DE-231	destroyer escort	12-09-43
—	LCC-1	landing craft — control	10-22-43
—	LCC-2	landing craft — control	10-22-43
—	LCC-3	landing craft — control	10-22-43
—	LCC-4	landing craft — control	10-22-43
—	LCC-5	landing craft — control	11-14-43
—	LCC-6	landing craft — control	11-14-43
—	LCC-7	landing craft — control	11-14-43
—	LCC-8	landing craft — control	11-14-43
—	LCC-9	landing craft — control	12-04-43
—	LCC-10	landing craft — control	12-04-43
—	LCC-11	landing craft — control	12-04-43
—	LCC-12	landing craft — control	12-04-43
Kinzer	APD-91	fast troop transport	12-09-43
Register	APD-92	fast troop transport	01-20-44
Brock	APD-93	fast troop transport	01-20-44
Roberts	APD-94	fast troop transport	02-11-44
Hobby	APD-95	fast troop transport	02-11-44
Edwards	APD-96	fast troop transport	02-19-44
Bristol	APD-97	fast troop transport	02-19-44
—	YSD-68	seaplane wrecking derrick	12-24-43
—	YSD-69	seaplane wrecking derrick	12-24-43
Truxtun	APD-98	fast troop transport	03-09-44
Upham	APD-99	fast troop transport	03-09-44
—	YSD-70	seaplane wrecking derrick	01-22-44
—	YSD-71	seaplane wrecking derrick	01-22-44
—	YSD-72	seaplane wrecking derrick	02-17-44
—	YSD-73	seaplane wrecking derrick	02-17-44
—	LCC-2-1	landing craft — control	01-22-44
—	LCC-2-2	landing craft — control	01-22-44
—	LCC-2-3	landing craft — control	02-05-44
—	LCC-2-4	landing craft — control	02-12-44
—	LCC-2-5	landing craft — control	02-19-44
—	LCC-2-6	landing craft — control	02-26-44
—	LCC-2-7	landing craft — control	03-04-44

Vessels Built By The Shipyard

Name	Number	Type	Launched
—	LCC-2-8	landing craft — control	03-11-44
—	LCC-2-9	landing craft — control	03-18-44
—	LCC-2-10	landing craft — control	03-25-44
—	LCC-2-11	landing craft — control	04-01-44
—	LCC-2-12	landing craft — control	04-08-44
—	LSM-126	medium landing ship	03-15-44
—	LSM-127	medium landing ship	03-15-44
—	LSM-128	medium landing ship	04-01-44
—	LSM-129	medium landing ship	04-01-44
—	LSM-130	medium landing ship	04-12-44
—	LSM-131	medium landing ship	04-12-44
—	LSM-132	medium landing ship	04-13-44
—	LSM-133	medium landing ship	04-13-44
—	LSM-134	medium landing ship	04-23-44
—	LSM-135	medium landing ship	04-23-44
—	LSM-136	medium landing ship	04-18-44
—	LSM-137	medium landing ship	04-18-44
—	LSM-138	medium landing ship	05-01-44
—	LSM-139	medium landing ship	05-01-44
—	LSM-140	medium landing ship	05-18-44
—	LSM-141	medium landing ship	05-18-44
—	LSM-142	medium landing ship	05-18-44
—	LSM-143	medium landing ship	05-10-44
—	LSM-144	medium landing ship	05-10-44
—	LSM-145	medium landing ship	05-14-44
—	LSM-146	medium landing ship	05-14-44
—	LSM-147	medium landing ship	05-14-44
—	LSM-148	medium landing ship	05-27-44
—	LSM-149	medium landing ship	05-27-44
—	LSM-150	medium landing ship	06-02-44
—	LSM-151	medium landing ship	06-02-44
—	LSM-152	medium landing ship	06-05-44
—	LSM-153	medium landing ship	06-05-44
—	LSM-154	medium landing ship	06-22-44
—	LSM-155	medium landing ship	06-19-44
—	LSM-156	medium landing ship	06-22-44
—	LSM-157	medium landing ship	06-19-44
—	LSM-158	medium landing ship	06-18-44
—	LSM-159	medium landing ship	06-18-44
—	LSM-160	medium landing ship	06-27-44
—	LSM-161	medium landing ship	06-27-44
—	LSM-162	medium landing ship	06-26-44
—	LSM-163	medium landing ship	06-26-44
—	LSM-164	medium landing ship	07-11-44
—	LSM-165	medium landing ship	07-11-44
—	LSM-166	medium landing ship	07-24-44
—	LSM-167	medium landing ship	07-24-44
—	LSM-168	medium landing ship	07-28-44
—	LSM-169	medium landing ship	07-28-44
—	LSM-170	medium landing ship	07-20-44
—	LSM-171	medium landing ship	07-20-44
—	LSM-172	medium landing ship	07-21-44
—	LSM-173	medium landing ship	07-21-44
—	LSM-174	medium landing ship	08-03-44
—	LSM-175	medium landing ship	08-03-44
—	LSM-176	medium landing ship	08-12-44
—	LSM-177	medium landing ship	08-12-44
—	LSM-178	medium landing ship	08-16-44
—	LSM-179	medium landing ship	08-16-44
—	LSM-180	medium landing ship	08-26-44
—	LSM-181	medium landing ship	08-26-44
—	LSM-182	medium landing ship	08-28-44
—	LSM-183	medium landing ship	08-28-44
—	LSM-184	medium landing ship	09-07-44

Vessels Built By The Shipyard

Name	Number	Type	Launched
—	LSM-185	medium landing ship	09-07-44
—	LSM-186	medium landing ship	09-05-44
—	LSM-187	medium landing ship	09-05-44
—	LSMR-188	medium landing ship-rocket	09-12-44
—	LSMR-189	medium landing ship-rocket	09-12-44
—	LSMR-190	medium landing ship-rocket	09-21-44
—	LSMR-191	medium landing ship-rocket	09-21-44
—	LSMR-192	medium landing ship-rocket	10-04-44
—	LSMR-193	medium landing ship-rocket	10-04-44
—	LSMR-194	medium landing ship-rocket	10-07-44
—	LSMR-195	medium landing ship-rocket	10-07-44
—	LSMR-196	medium landing ship-rocket	10-12-44
—	LSMR-197	medium landing ship-rocket	10-12-44
—	LSMR-198	medium landing ship-rocket	10-14-44
—	LSMR-199	medium landing ship-rocket	10-14-44
—	LSM-200	medium landing ship	10-17-44
—	LSM-295	medium landing ship	10-17-44
—	LSM-296	medium landing ship	10-30-44
—	LSM-297	medium landing ship	10-30-44
—	LSM-298	medium landing ship	11-13-44
—	LSM-299	medium landing ship	11-13-44
—	LSM-300	medium landing ship	11-19-44
—	LSM-301	medium landing ship	11-19-44
—	LSM-302	medium landing ship	11-14-44
—	LSM-303	medium landing ship	11-14-44
—	LSM-304	medium landing ship	11-27-44
—	LSM-305	medium landing ship	11-27-44
—	LSM-306	medium landing ship	11-14-44
—	LSM-307	medium landing ship	11-14-44
—	LSM-308	medium landing ship	12-09-44
—	LSM-309	medium landing ship	12-09-44
—	LSM-389	medium landing ship	12-12-44
—	LSM-390	medium landing ship	12-12-44
—	LSM-391	medium landing ship	12-17-44
—	LSM-392	medium landing ship	12-17-44
—	LSM-393	medium landing ship	12-29-44
—	LSM-394	medium landing ship	12-29-44
—	LSM-395	medium landing ship	01-02-45
—	LSM-396	medium landing ship	01-02-45
—	LSM-397	medium landing ship	01-06-45
—	LSM-398	medium landing ship	01-06-45
—	LSM-399	medium landing ship	01-18-45
—	LSM-400	medium landing ship	01-18-45
—	LSMR-401	medium landing ship-rocket	01-22-45
—	LSMR-402	medium landing ship-rocket	01-22-45
—	LSMR-403	medium landing ship-rocket	01-26-45
—	LSMR-404	medium landing ship-rocket	01-26-45
—	LSMR-405	medium landing ship-rocket	02-06-45
—	LSMR-406	medium landing ship-rocket	02-06-45
—	LSMR-407	medium landing ship-rocket	02-12-45
—	LSMR-408	medium landing ship-rocket	02-12-45
—	LSMR-409	medium landing ship-rocket	02-18-45
—	LSMR-410	medium landing ship-rocket	02-18-45
—	LSMR-411	medium landing ship-rocket	02-25-45
—	LSMR-412	medium landing ship-rocket	02-25-45
—	LSM-413	medium landing ship	03-03-45
—	LSM-553	medium landing ship	03-03-45
—	LSM-554	medium landing ship	03-22-45
—	LSM-555	medium landing ship	03-22-45
—	LSM-556	medium landing ship	04-10-45
—	LSM-557	medium landing ship	04-10-45
—	LSM-558	medium landing ship	04-28-45
Tidewater	AD-31	destroyer tender	06-30-45
Bryce Canyon	AD-36	destroyer tender	03-07-46

Acknowledgements

This book is the result of the efforts of many people. These efforts began when the Charleston Naval Shipyard chapter of the Naval Civilian Administrators Association undertook the project to produce a shipyard history more than five years ago.

Many members of the association contributed to the book. Jack T. Day had hundreds of historical photographs assembled and kept the project alive over a several-year period when little was accomplished. He also assisted in preparation of the book in many other ways. Walden Lown did extensive research on the early Navy Yard and put together the foundation for much of the text. Palmer W. Olliff provided many historical photographs, invaluable assistance and much encouragement to the author. Jack Riley strongly supported the project, both as president of the local chapter of the NCAA and as the author's boss while the book was being written. Jim Beltz took care of many details related to publishing the book. Other members of the association who contributed in many ways included "R. J." Argenzio-West, Tom Cooper, Larry Driggers, Mike Geffen, E. W. Hardwicke, E. A. "Red" Rice, Carroll Smith, and Tom Tidwell.

The other shipyard management organizations also provided considerable support in the project. The local chapter of Federal Managers Association, led by President J. D. Rogers, provided indispensable financial backing for publishing of the book.

Nor would publication of the book by the NCAA have been possible without the help of the shipyard Employee Services Association. Willie Givens, Gloria Bell and Howard Quillan, in particular, deserve special thanks for their considerable effort related to the selling and distribution of the book.

Many other shipyard employees also contributed to the book. Frances Tate carefully proofread the manuscript and made many helpful suggestions that improved the text. Mike Shumake and Sally Lawson of the Shipyard Public Affairs Office provided much assistance. The photographers of the CNS photo lab — E. D. Stello, Bonnell Black, Tony Diz, and Bob Kay — produced many fine photographs for the book. Others who provided historical material or helped in other ways included A. F. "Pee Wee" Ackerman, Janice Amell, Kama Bentley, Jimmie Budds, Dee Cercopely, Bob Davidson, Eugene Davis, Bob Foster, Elbert Hodges, Hayden C. Hooper, Elva Holt, Sandy Hutto, W. S. Kearse, Wayne Knight, Jim Meherg, Jimmie Mizzell, Charles Mulligan, Ken Palka, Nancy Price, Raymond Roberts, John Sneed, Raymond Tucker, James B. Vickers, Diane Walker, Vernelle Williams and Cynthia Wilson. Linda Finger did her usual splendid job in typing the manuscript and helped track down much of the historical material.

Captain W. J. Mahony, USN (Retired), who was Shipyard Commander when the NCAA began preparations for the book, was a staunch supporter of the project during its initial phase.

The book would not have been possible without the assistance of the people of the Naval Historical Center. Agnes Hoover, in particular, was a great help, locating and providing many photographs of ships associated with the shipyard over the years. Also, a number of people at Naval Sea Systems Command devoted considerable effort to reviewing Chapter Seven and the modern photographs to ensure that they were suitable for publication. Pat Dooling of the Charleston Naval Base Public Affairs Office helped with the project in many ways.

Several other people reviewed the manuscript and made many useful suggestions. J. Percival Petit of the Isle of Palms and Captain John T. Pierce, USN (Retired) of Summerville suggested a number of improvements to the first chapter. J. Douglas Donehue of the *News and Courier* also made several recommendations which substantially improved the book. Mal J. Collet, Director of The Citadel Museum, kindly reviewed the manuscript. Isabella Leland generously made available her extensive research notes on the frigate *John Adams*. Paul Allen, president of the Charleston Naval Shipyard Federal Credit Union, was a strong supporter of the project and helped considerably with efforts to publicize and market the book.

Although no bibliography is included with the book, several hundred different primary and secondary sources were consulted in preparation of the text and legends for the pictures. Particularly valuable were Dr. Lyon G. Tyler, Jr.'s history of the Charleston Naval Base and the *Dictionary of American Naval Fighting Ships* produced by the Naval Historical Center.

The material in Chapter Three on Norman Rockwell was taken from his autobiography, *Norman Rockwell, My Adventures as an Illustrator, as Told to Thomas Rockwell*, and was used with the permission of Thomas Rockwell.

Other organizations and individuals who contributed material included:

Mrs. James H. Boswell of Summerville
The R. L. Bryan Co. — Alan McNeel
Captain William Izard Bull, USN (Retired)
The Carolina Art Association, Gibbs Art Gallery — Martha Severens
The Charleston Museum — Sharon Bennett
The Charleston Naval Shipyard Federal Credit Union — Sharon Pastorius
The Charleston *News and Courier*
The Citadel Museum — Mal J. Collet
George Collins of North Charleston
Raymond Deneaux of Charleston
Samuel F. Fennessy of Charleston
A. A. Ilderton of North Charleston
Llewellyn A. Izlar of Charleston
Edgar W. Jones of Summerville
The Library of Congress
Sean McNeil of Hanahan
The Mariner's Museum, Newport News, VA — Roger T. Crew Jr.
The National Archives
The Norman Rockwell Museum of Stockbridge, Mass. — Laurie Norton Moffatt and Linda Russell
The National Park Service, Fort Moultrie National Monument — David Ruth
The Peabody Museum of Salem — Kathy Flynn
Robert W. Sanderson of Williamsburg, VA
William M. Sullivan of Mt. Pleasant
The South Carolina Historical Society
U. S. Army Corps of Engineers, Charleston District — Marlene Judy
U. S. Naval Academy Museum — R. F. Sumrall
U. S. Naval Base, Charleston — Public Affairs Office

Photographs not otherwise credited are official U. S. Navy photos, most provided by the Naval Historical Center.

INDEX